To

From

WAITING
- in -
WONDER

GROWING IN FAITH WHILE
YOU'RE EXPECTING

A DEVOTIONAL JOURNAL

CATHERINE CLAIRE LARSON

COUNTRYMAN®

THOMAS NELSON
Since 1798

NASHVILLE   DALLAS   MEXICO CITY   RIO DE JANEIRO

Published in Nashville, Tennessee, by Thomas Nelson. Thomas Nelson is a registered trademark of HarperCollins Christian Publishing, Inc.

Represented by Andrea Heinecke of Alive Communications.

Cover design by Mary Hooper, Milkglass Creative.

Thomas Nelson titles may be purchased in bulk for educational, business, fund-raising, or sales promotional use. For information, please e-mail SpecialMarkets@ ThomasNelson.com.

ISBN-13: 978-1-4003-2107-0

Printed in China

18 19 20 WAI 8 7

www.thomasnelson.com

*To my beloved husband, Mark, and to our
two sons, Luke and Isaiah, who continue
to fill my heart with wonder and joy.*

Contents

Seize the Wait: Drawing Near to God in This Sacred Season of Expectancy

$\mathcal{L}$ ight didn't stream through stained glass windows. No preacher took the pulpit. No choir raised angelic voices. Yet no worship service could have been any sweeter than the one housed within those sterile hospital walls. Nothing could have been more instinctive, natural, and right than to worship God in that sacred moment.

I expected him to come with wailing, fists clenched in rage. Instead, he entered this world with eyes open wide in quiet wonder. Until that moment when I clutched a warm, squirming life naked to my chest, I had never known such raw joy. He pulled a tiny fist to his mouth as his steely blue eyes met my own. We stared at one another, him blinking thoughtfully, me babbling words of delight and praise—my speech suddenly reduced to stammered fragments. I admired his long slender fingers, his soft skin, and his head of downy dark hair. And my eyes bounced between his and my husband's, like light dancing on the water on a still day.

It was the wee hours of the morning by then. And when I suddenly remembered it was Sunday, nothing could have felt more fitting. For when you've prayed like Hannah and been given a gift of grace like Samuel, holding that long-awaited treasure makes your heart swell with the gratitude and worship of a thousand Sundays. And I knew deep within that this gift was a gift that could only be quickly offered back to the Giver in praise and adoration.

That day I did not raise my hands in worship—I lowered them to form a cradle for the miracle that had been entrusted to me. I worshiped my Creator with eyes wide open in wonder.

As I think back on the day my son was born and that amazing spontaneous worship service, I realize that for at least nine months, God had been preparing my heart for that culmination in praise.

THE CREATOR ACTS

Biology has always captivated me, and from the time I found out I was pregnant, I'd been poring over books, tracing the development of my baby. I loved learning how Baby was measuring up each week as I took an imaginary cruise up the produce aisle: pomegranate seed, blueberry, lime, clementine, orange, mango, cantaloupe, and watermelon. I would read something that amazed me and meditate on it for days: my baby was perhaps already dreaming in the womb; his eyes could sense light and he would turn to it; his ear was already being primed to show preference for my voice. And with every passing milestone, my heart seemed to grow, swelling with worship, just as my belly was swelling with life.

These weren't random, inexplicable wonders caused by chance or a freak survival-of-the-fittest phenomenon. *God* was forming my child, fearfully and wonderfully fashioning this little life day by day. And the intricacies of design that I was reading about were *His* intricacies, *His* careful hand, *His* perfect timing, and *His* marvelous creativity.

Meanwhile, in my own personal times with the Lord, passages from His Word were coming alive to me like never before. As I reread the stories of Sarah, Hannah, Elizabeth, and Mary, I grew more keenly aware of the incredible high calling of motherhood. These stories weren't merely about expectant mothers; these stories were about God using mothers to build and further His kingdom. And as I felt the first flutters of life, I also felt the sacred honor of taking the mantle of motherhood from these great women who'd gone before me.

Journaling has never come easily to me, but during those days, I kept adding to a book of love notes for my baby. In the book I wrote down milestones: the day I learned I was pregnant, how the baby's father and I shared the news, the first time I saw the heartbeat, the first time I felt Baby move, and more. I recorded prayers for my baby: for his physical heart to grow strong and his spiritual heart to come to worship God one day. I told him how my own heart kept stretching wider with love for him and deeper with love for God because of him. I had the stretch marks to prove it!

So when Luke Aaron Larson came quietly in the early hours of the Lord's Day that spring of 2010, nestling so naturally into the arms that had been aching to hold him, nothing could have culminated that long-awaited moment better than praise. No one needed to cue me to lift my heart to the Lord. My heart responded as so many hearts have in ages past, saying, "It is right, and a good and joyful thing . . . to give thanks to you, Father Almighty, Creator of heaven and earth."[1]

Now, less than two years later, as God is once again forming another fearfully and wonderfully made creation inside me, my heart yearns to come alongside other expectant mothers in this sacred time of waiting. Nothing would please me more than—by God's grace—to encourage you in the practices and habits of the heart that will make that birth day into a holy celebration.

But that is really only the beginning. For that birth day should be not just a worship service of praise for whom God has made and brought into your arms, but in a very real sense, also a holy commissioning service.

God has chosen you for a sacred calling: to nurture a particular soul, exquisitely unique and immeasurably important. Our Father in heaven has handpicked you to mother this exact child, the one who began as a single cell, the one whose very odds of existence boggle the mind, and the one who will be so strangely like you and yet so strangely different.

THE JOURNEY NEARS

Whether you're a first-time mom or a seasoned veteran of mother-hood, God graciously gives each mother nine months. Nine months to prepare for a sacred journey—a journey you will be taking with this particular child, to nurture, to disciple, and to teach about Jesus.

Nine months isn't very long to prepare for such a journey. But God knows you will never truly be ready for the rigorous demands of motherhood. If you were, you would have no need to lean on Him in dependence, no need to keep your own eyes on Jesus, your Guide. Though you will never be completely ready for motherhood, God longs to help you—He longs for you to make the most of this waiting time by drawing nearer to Him.

Seeing pregnancy as the preparation time for such deeply spiritual work can feel overwhelming. You may not have yet shared the news that you're expecting with even your closest friends. Or you may not know anyone willing or able to walk with you during this time when life is drastically changing by the minute. Maybe your best friend is struggling with infertility, or your mom lives miles away. Perhaps your sister is single, and your spouse, try as he may, can't fully understand the hormonal roller coaster you are riding.

But the God who made you and the One who is forming this child within you longs to walk with you during this sacred season of waiting. He wants to share in what you're feeling. He wants to open up truths from His Word that will comfort you and challenge you to become even more of the woman—and the mother—He designed you to be. And He wants to awaken you to the wonder of this miraculous creation He is even now forming within you.

It's my sincere hope that through this journal your pregnancy can be a time of adopting certain practices that will shape your life and the life of your child forever: meditating on Scripture as a means to personal metamorphosis, foregoing anxiety in favor of prayer, and journaling as a tool for remembering God's faithfulness. I pray that as these devotions lead you to linger over the details of God's amazing handiwork in creation, you will also find your sense of wonder renewed and, with it, your heart revived to praise.

To that end, in the pages of this beautiful devotional journal, *Waiting in Wonder*, you will find daily readings and Scripture passages brought together just for you and for this special season of your life. You will also find helpful prompts that lead you to record your emotions, significant milestones, prayers, and love notes to your baby. What a precious gift to be able to give to your son or daughter one day—the gift of knowing you and the love you had for him or her even before you nuzzled his or her life in your arms.

The book is arranged by weeks of pregnancy. Most health-care providers in the United States calculate the typical forty-week pregnancy from a woman's last menstrual period. Ironically enough that means that in the first two weeks of your forty-week pregnancy, you aren't even pregnant yet. Usually sometime between that second and third week conception occurs. And then there is a two-week window of time that passes before most women even know they are pregnant. For that reason I've begun the devotional journal at the fifth week of pregnancy, the time when most women have just discovered the exciting news.

For each week I've provided a development summary with points for prayer and praise, a memory verse taken from one of the devotional passages in the week ahead, and four days of devotional material. You may like doing these devotionals Monday through Friday when the daily routine is a little more normalized. On weekends, consider going deeper into the Word with one of the Scripture passages that spoke to you during the week. For most readers a day will pass here and there when you don't get to a reading. Don't worry; just pick back up on the week of pregnancy you are in.

On most days, I've provided a couple of writing prompts. The first prompt is usually designed to help you meditate further on the truth from God's Word that has been presented that day. The second will typically lead you to record something for your baby, perhaps a prayer, a memory, a milestone, or a little note of love.

Perhaps you're reading this introduction in a bookstore while perusing the myriad of titles on pregnancy, and you're contemplating quietly putting this book back on the shelf. You may be thinking, *Who has time for this?* After all there are so many other things to do right now—from finding the best doctor or midwife, to choosing the right stroller, to picking the perfect name, to painting the nursery. But before you move on with your "to do" list, I encourage you not to neglect the most important thing you can do for both yourself and your child: strengthening your relationship with God *today.* Ten years from now, you may not remember the brand of stroller you had, and your son or daughter will not remember the nursery's color, but both of you will be forever shaped by the way you walked with God and the way you embraced and prepared for the calling of motherhood. And your child will also have a lasting reminder of your love for God and for him or her in the very pages of this journal.

The Calling Awaits

You are an exquisite creation made by the living God, handpicked for one of His most important callings. Embrace this season of waiting in life by entering deeper into the wonder of who God is, the miracle He's forming within you, and the dignity and importance of the work He has laid before you.

My hope for you is that when your son or daughter is finally in your arms, just nine short months from now, these daily readings and the prayers, praises, and love you've recorded in the pages of this journal will culminate in one of the purest moments of worship you have ever known. I also hope that as you lift your heart to God in praise and cradle that precious life in your arms, you will have been prepared in deep and profound ways for the high and holy calling of motherhood.

Visit CatherineClaireLarson.com for a free download of *Waiting in Wonder* memory verses. Carry them with you, put them on your bathroom mirror, or even tuck them in your hospital bag when labor draws near.

Your Awakening Wonder:
First Trimester

The Wonder Within

Only about two weeks have passed since conception, and already there's an amazing miracle unfolding inside of you. What began as a single fertilized egg has made the harrowing journey down a fallopian tube and implanted in the lush lining of your uterus. Cells have multiplied exponentially since conception, putting your little one at about the size of a pomegranate seed (0.13 in.) this week. Already three distinct layers have formed that will give rise to all the organs and tissues in the body. The neural tube (the precursor to the spinal cord, backbone, brain, and nerves) forms this week, but has not yet closed. And perhaps most stunning of all, God will cue a tiny heart to begin beating.

Unless you have an irregular cycle, you have already missed your period. And by God's amazing design, hormones in your body have sounded an alarm for drastic changes to begin occurring. Those hormones signal the body not to shed the lining of the uterus, but instead to remain full to protect the life that's embedded and to begin forming the vital organs such as the placenta, which will nourish your little one for the next nine months. These hormones and other changes in your body are also quite possibly already making you feel nauseous, averse to certain smells, emotional, and exhausted. Every symptom, however, is just another reminder that, to the glory of God, a little life has begun to form inside you and your life will never be the same.

Points for Prayer and Praise

- Praise God for conception—even under optimum conditions there is only a 10 to 15 percent chance of conceiving on any given cycle.
- Life is still extremely tenuous at this point; pray for the neural tube to begin forming properly and for the heart to begin beating.
- As the discovery of your pregnancy sinks in, ask God to help you as you process this life-changing information. And ask that you will come to fully accept and rejoice in both the news itself and the hidden wisdom of God's perfect timing.

Mommy's Memory Verse:

Sons are a heritage from the LORD,
children a reward from him.

PSALM 127:3

Date:
6/10/19

Intimacy with Christ

Each heart knows its own bitterness,
and no one else can share its joy.

PROVERBS 14:10

You squint at the small window of your home pregnancy test. Three minutes never passed so slowly. Then—could it really be? Perhaps your plus sign came after years of negative ones and no words could possibly contain your joy. Or maybe your positive came only six weeks after having a new baby, or maybe it's only five days into starting your dream job. No matter your situation, you're excited, but you can't shake your shock. And whether the news makes you feel like squealing with delight or wheezing with anxiety, there is One who understands.

The intimacy you share with Christ is absolutely unique. No matter how close you might be to someone, no one understands you the way He does. He created you. He knows every millisecond of your past and every detail of your circumstances. No mother, sister, friend, or spouse will ever understand you so completely or be able to rejoice with you so wholly. But God does.

Rejoice today that you have access to the most beautiful and intimate relationship available: a relationship with Christ. If you feel like shouting your joy from the mountaintops, He exults with you! If your eyes are brimming with tears and you need someone to hear your worries, He stands ready with open arms. No matter your response to this news, you have the perfect One to share with you in this moment: to rejoice with you, to comfort you, or to whisper that all things happen in His perfect time.

Well, I'm actually 7 weeks, I bought this journal a little late, so need to catch up :) but Lord, I am very excited! Thank you for choosing me to be a mother to one of your precious children. Also maybe a little nervous for the baby's development, and the unknowns of pregnancy and motherhood coming up... but I just give all of that to you in your hands. I know you are in control. Thank you for the peace you have washed over me ♡.

Justin and I took a trip to Maui, w/out birth control, in hopes this could be our time to conceive... and sure enough it was! One week after getting back, and being very tired and emotional all week long, I was one day late so I took the test! Boom! Positive! I was overjoyed and shocked, I immediately began praising God, and praying for the baby ♡. I told Justin the next day (caz he was at work!) He cried and laughed & was overjoyed!

Date:
_6/10/19_____

The Blessing of Children

Sons are a heritage from the LORD,
children a reward from him.

PSALM 127:3

*F*lip through prime time's sitcoms, and it won't take you long to absorb what our culture thinks about children: they drain your love life, your wallet, your independence, your patience, and your sanity. If there's one message you probably won't get, it's the one God wants you to hear: children are a blessing.

Yes, you will be changing diapers and cutting coupons. Yes, date nights with your husband will get harder and time to yourself scarcer. But God does not see children as a liability. He calls them a reward.

At the very heart of God is relationship. Father, Son, and Holy Spirit have eternally and blissfully enjoyed togetherness. Perfect relationship overflows with love. And at the beginning of time, love overflowed in creation. God created man in His image. He created us to be like Him and to be in the process of becoming more and more like Him.

When God gives us children, He gives us some of His best gifts. He gives us the gift of relationship. He gives us the opportunity to know one of life's deepest joys: serving another with selfless love. And He gives us a taste of the delight there is in creation, of the delight there is in seeing another made in one's image, of the delight there is in seeing another grow in that family resemblance. These are His good gifts.

Ask God to show you any ways in which the culture's dim view of children has tainted your own views. Ask God to make the things that are sweet to Him sweet to you. Write a prayer of thanks for the blessing God is giving you in the form of this little life growing inside you.

Wow, Lord, this is beautiful! Thank you! and ya, I needed to hear it ☺. Culture has painted that in a negative light. But that is selfish and distrustful thinking! Thank you for the wonderful Reward you have blessed me with! To experience this kind of love and relationship will only draw me closer to you! ♥ Thank you Jesus!

Dear Little One,

You are a priceless gift. As I look out into the future, I see my life blessed in so many ways because of you. Some of the blessings I look forward to most are:

- Snuggles, laughes, and giggles so genuine and pure ♥
- The love we will have for each other
- Being needed by you ♥
- The privalege of introducing you to Jesus
- Giving you good gifts and a good life
- understanding better how God loves me, through to way I unconditionally love you!

The Heart Awakens

From the place of His dwelling He looks
on all the inhabitants of the earth;
He fashions their hearts individually;
He considers all their works.

PSALM 33:14–15 NKJV

*O*nly weeks have passed since conception, and already something so mysterious is happening inside you that scientists themselves struggle to understand it. Within that poppy seed–sized embryo, cells begin migrating and fuse to form a tube. Spontaneously one of those cells jolts awake and begins to beat. That beat starts a chain reaction. The cells nearby begin dancing to the same rhythm. And in the weeks ahead this tube will divide to form the four chambers of the heart.

Scientists are still trying to plumb the mysteries of the heart. While the brain later controls how fast the heart beats, the heartbeat itself is initiated spontaneously. What awakens the heart? Perhaps the better question is, who awakens the heart? wow!

God forms the hearts of all. He has woven into the DNA of these cells a message that tells them precisely when to awaken. He forms the surrounding cells to begin beating to the same rhythm. Before any of us have lived a single day, God already knows precisely how many beats each heart will be given in its lifetime. Whether those beats are few or well into the billions, we can trust that the God who orchestrates the very first heartbeat has a purpose for each heart He forms.

Stop for a moment and meditate on the wonder of a God who can create a heart. If He can coordinate the timing of microscopic cells to begin beating, why do we doubt His timing in any area of our lives? If He can cause a single cell to jolt awake, how much more is He capable of bringing something out of nothing in our lives? In what areas do you need to trust Him more? Affirm that He is worthy of your trust.

Trust - yes! This was my "word" for 2019! I know I have a hard time with this sometimes, I'm getting better, but still I repent of my sporatic worry... which is not trusting you. I think it's just hard for me to fathom the paradox of your sovereignty amongst human free-will! you are more than worthy of ALL of me and of ALL of my trust! Thank you Lord for daily reminders of your goodness, love, & control! ♡.

Dear Little One,

While God is at work forming your physical heart, I am praying for your spiritual heart. Here are a few of the things I am asking God for on your behalf:

• Lord may this child know you, and have the capacity to understand how deep, and wide, is your love for them!
• May you find your Identity, your strength, and your purpose in God alone!
• May you grow in wisdom, and seek the Lord & his kingdom above all else ♡.

Amen

Let It Be

"I am the Lord's servant," Mary answered.
"May it be to me as you have said."

LUKE 1:38

God gives us an intimate window to the most important pregnancy announcement of all time. Mary didn't squint at a home pregnancy test. Instead, an angel appeared to her and told her that soon she would be expecting. But this wasn't any ordinary pregnancy; she would be carrying the Son of God. While there could be no greater honor, there certainly was a lot for her to feel anxious about. After all, she was not married, she was very young, and her story would be totally unbelievable to most around her. How would Joseph react? And what's worse, the penalty for her pregnancy could have been stoning. Talk about a crisis pregnancy!

But while Mary certainly had every right to respond with shock, fear, misgivings, or even depression, she modeled for us an attitude of total submission to the will of God. She said, in essence, "Let it be." She said "amen" to God's providence and His plan for her life.

Whether the news of your pregnancy was met with intense joy or intense anxiety, God calls each of us to come to a place of acceptance. None of us knows what the future holds. But if we are His daughters, we know that He has allowed this pregnancy as part of His plan for us. Can you say to God, "I am your servant; let it be"?

Pregnancy and a new baby bring great joy, but they also bring adjustments, hardships, and sacrifices. As you think about what these will be in your life, take them each to God in prayer. How does God use sacrifices and difficulties in our lives to make us more like Him?

- No longer just about me and my schedule / "to-do's"
- May have to ask others for help
- Costs money
- Becoming more selfless all around really!

Lord, I know you are totally in control, so I don't need to worry or freak out, though I know I will sometimes, but help me to not do it so often! It's very clear how kids help us to become more like you, so thank you for this

Dear Little One, honor and opportunity. I need you Lord! Help me raise and steward this baby well!

I want you to know that not only are you accepted into my life, you are welcomed joyfully. When I think about you joining our family, I rejoice and imagine . . .

how much everyone is going love love you like crazy! I mean a ridiculous amount! You are one lucky little ducky coming into this wild, crazy, huge, fun, loving family ♡. Try not to get a big ego, haha, cuz we will all be obsessed w/ you! I imagine all the funny / sweet and sassy/naughty things you'll say and do! I imagine the way you will discover the world w/ wonder ♡ I imagine your little heartfelt prayers to your Creator and your faith! I imagine our hugs and snuggles, and special mommy dates when daddy's @ work... and also visiting daddy @ the fire station!

You have a really cool dad! ♡

WEEK 6

The Wonder Within

You may think you have a busy week ahead, but it's nothing compared to what's going on with your little sweet pea this week. And speaking of sweet pea, that's roughly the size of your little one right now, measuring in at a quarter of an inch (from crown to rump). Your little pea in the pod is busy, busy: eyes, ears, mouth, chin, cheeks, and jaw are all beginning to form. In addition to these kissable parts, tissue that will become lungs, kidneys, intestines, liver, a pituitary gland, muscles, and bones are forming. Arm and leg buds appear as well. How amazing is it that God has programmed your little one's DNA with all the information necessary to create the human mind and body!

God is at work in you also. Already the hormone HCG (the one that turned your pregnancy test positive) is signaling your body to increase blood flow. Your uterus—the home God designed for your baby—is growing and beginning to press into your bladder, which is one of the reasons, along with increased kidney efficiency, that you are likely running to the bathroom around the clock. Morning sickness may be starting. If it is, take heart in the fact that it is a sure sign that your body is preparing for this new little life. Lean into the loving arms of God, who cares for you and will see you through the days ahead.

Points for Prayer and Praise

- If you are already beginning to experience morning sickness or other pregnancy symptoms, praise God for the tangible reminder that He is at work within your body, producing this new life. If you've yet to feel any symptoms, thank God for the reprieve.

- Pray for your little one as the neural tube, which connects the brain and spinal cord, closes this week. This is a critical point in baby's development.

- Pray for your little one to one day come to know Jesus as his or her personal Savior.

Mommy's Memory Verse

*"Before I formed you in
the womb I knew you."*

Jeremiah 1:5

My Spirit Rejoices

*Mary said: "My soul glorifies the Lord
and my spirit rejoices in God my Savior."*

Luke 1:46–47

*L*ast week, we looked at the most important pregnancy announcement of all time. We saw Mary's example of acceptance even in the face of difficult news. But Mary didn't just submit to the will of God; she rejoiced in it, despite whatever hardship it might bring to her own life. She moved beyond mere submission to a sacrifice of praise.

As she praised God, she called to mind His mercies in the past generations, His strength to bring down and raise up rulers, and His faithfulness to those who love Him. She saw what God was doing in her life as part of the larger picture of God's work in the world.

If the news of your pregnancy was difficult, Mary provides an example of moving beyond mere acceptance to joy. But even if the news of your pregnancy was wonderful news to you, have you seen it as part of a bigger picture? Have you seen this gift of life as part of the unfolding story of the mercy and faithfulness of God? Have you seen this little life as perhaps part of the new story of what God is doing in this world? Have you rejoiced in this news as representing something bigger than just you and your personal happiness? If not, it's time to let your soul glorify God and let your spirit rejoice.

Mary rehearsed various aspects of the character of God that are reflected in the news of her pregnancy (Luke 1:46–55). What aspects of God's character do you see reflected in the news of your own pregnancy?

- His design and intense creativity
- His love.
- His perfect timing
- His heart for relationship displayed through family
- His joy and delight in us

Mary's song of praise, called "The Magnificat", is perhaps one of the most well-known and beloved outbursts of praise in the Bible. Write your own prayer of rejoicing, or even song of praise, here as you reflect on the news of the life growing inside you.

Thank you Lord! you have blessed me, and chosen me for the high honor of motherhood! You placed this desire firmly on my heart, and you have followed through! You are the ultimate giver of good gifts! Restore, rejuvinate, and strengthen my faith through the eyes and childlike faith of my baby! Thank you for this wonderful, and beautiful opportunity! Help me to allow myself to fully relish in the joy of this time!

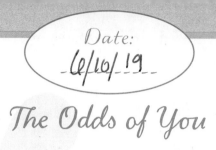

The Odds of You

*"Before I formed you in
the womb I knew you."*

JEREMIAH 1:5

*H*ave you ever stopped to consider the odds of your existence? A friend recently told me how her parents met. Her father, a native of Alabama, met her mother, a French Canadian, sitting poolside on the East Coast. Her mother spoke only a handful of English phrases, but it didn't deter her father from asking her out. Sometime later the man traveled to Quebec to visit someone else, but remembered the girl he'd met. On a whim, he drove to the local Ford dealership and in his characteristic Southern drawl asked if anyone knew her. He was pointed toward her home. An impromptu date turned into an invitation from her family to stay for a week. And three years later, despite the odds, the two were married.

Now multiply unlikely scenarios like this millions of times over. In order for you to exist, each of your ancestral grandfathers had to have met each of your ancestral grandmothers at just the right time. Had they started their family earlier or later, you would not be—or at least would not be you. Likewise, had your life unfolded differently, the child growing within you would not be.

But here's the thing: there are no odds about it. God knew you and your baby before He laid the foundations of the world. He had already planned you both, and every circumstance it would take to get you here.

When you consider that God planned you before He even made Adam and Eve, how does it make you feel? And if you are God's child, you were chosen in Him before time (Ephesians 1:4). Offer God thanks for how He orchestrated every detail of life not only so that you would exist but also so that, in His good time, you call Him Lord.

Wow, Lord, honestly I never really powered the fact that you had me in mind even before making Adam and Eve! Wow! That is truly amazing and just speaks to your vastness and attention to detail. There's a lot up in the air here on earth, but it's comforting to know that someday we will understand! But you are God, and your ways are higher! :)

Dear Little One,

I want to tell you how I met your father . . .

I was 18, and daddy was 21. I was a waitress at Sammy's woodfired pizza and daddy sat at one of my tables with 2 friends. At the end of the night (his 2 friends had left) he formaly introduced himself, and gave me my tip in person. Inside the rolled up money was a small card w/ his name + phone number...and it said "Maybe sometime you can join me for a Sunday" (I had brought their table a messy sunday) anyway and the rest is history! Now here you are 7 yrs later

New Creation

Jesus declared, "I tell you the truth,
no one can see the kingdom of
God unless he is born again."

JOHN 3:3

*I*sn't it marvelous to imagine your future baby? This boy or girl will be unlike any the world has ever seen. Sure, you will see similarities to you and your spouse and perhaps even relatives from further up the family tree. But those similarities don't undermine the plain fact that you have been allowed to participate in one of the most amazing miracles of all: new creation.

When Jesus spoke with Nicodemus, a Pharisee who asked what he must do to be saved, Jesus told him that he must be born again. At its most basic level, to be "born again" is to be a new creation. This isn't just a reformation or renovation of something old. It is to be made entirely new.

I would be remiss if I didn't ask you: Are you born again? Have you ever truly repented of your sins (turned from them) and believed in Jesus Christ as your only means of salvation? His death on the cross in your place (dying the death you deserved) pays the penalty for your sin if you will believe in Him. And because God raised Christ from the dead, we can be certain that He will also raise us from our sins, giving us new spiritual life and the hope of eternal life after we die.

Are you born again? If this is something new to you, take time now to pray and turn to God in repentance and belief. Then document this momentous new birth here. If, however, this is something that has already happened in your life, tell your future son or daughter about your rebirth.

I grew up learning about God, but I really made it my own after age 18. After a breakup and living the typical "college lifestyle" that did not satisfy, I needed MORE! and I became His, and my life was forever changed." I actually met daddy 3 months after this Rebirth ♥.

Repentance and belief are not simply the gate by which we come to Christ. They are the everyday business of the spiritual life. We never get past these basics of the Christian life. This is how we come to Christ and how we grow as Christians. Write a prayer for yourself and your future little one that your lives will be marked by the everyday rhythm of repentance and belief.

Lord, I know that I am not perfect, and this little bean won't be either. But we are made rightous in you! May we live our lives daily surrendered to you ... aware and repentant of our wrongdoings, and Believing that you covered them all.'

Date:
_6/12/19._

A New Thing

*"Behold, I will do a new thing, now it
shall spring forth; shall you not know
it? I will even make a road in the
wilderness and rivers in the desert."*

ISAIAH 43:19 NKJV

Perhaps you've already begun to feel the signs of pregnancy. In fact, the signs may have given it away before you took a pregnancy test. You're exhausted. You're running to the bathroom every few minutes. Your breasts are tender. You're nauseous. And the slightest smell seems overpowering. Aside from a bit of bloating, no one could tell by looking at you that you are pregnant. But for many women, small signs pointing to this new reality begin early.

In the Old Testament book of Isaiah, God's people were exiled in Babylon. They were weary of being oppressed and so far from home. But God was at work. He was about to do a new thing in their midst. He was bringing salvation, and He told them that there were signs of it—small but perceptible signs—all around them. In Isaiah 43 God alluded to the exodus and how He brought the people out of Egypt, but He also told the people to "forget the former things" (verse 18) because this new thing He was doing among them was so much greater. The words here were pointing to a twofold reality: God would bring His people out of physical exile from Babylon, and then He would bring them even greater salvation through Christ, who would lead them out of spiritual exile.

In the Old Testament God's people were first enslaved in Egypt for nearly four hundred years, then in Babylon later. Physical captivity, exile, and all the hardships they endured became a metaphor for what it means to be in sin. How did Christ redeem you from the bondage of sin when He saved you? What shackles came off?

I felt peace, Joy, and love. Life had meaning and I no longer suffered in Apathy. I have security and confidence in my Identity and myself. I can love more genuinely.

How does this little one represent a new thing God is doing in your life? In what ways will your life be different because of him or her?

I now have the privilege of a very important job: loving and training someone up in the ways of the lord. My priorities are different now. This is something that I need God desperately to help me to do. More structure & routine will need to be cultivated in my life.

WEEK 7

The Wonder Within

Go ahead, dream about those adorable little hands that will clasp your own and those tiny feet to cover in kisses—because this week God is orchestrating the emergence of both. This is another big week developmentally for your little one, who is about the size of a blueberry now (0.51 in.). By the end of the week, he or she will have almost doubled in length. Much of the current growth is going on in the brain where one hundred nerve cells develop each minute. (But you already knew your blueberry was smart, right?)

Speaking of growing, you are doing a bit of your own: your uterus has doubled in size since conception. Meanwhile, you may also begin to notice your bra fitting more snugly. If you've noticed any breast tenderness, it's because God is already preparing your body to nourish your baby outside the womb with the perfect sustenance for his or her growing body.

Feeling like you're an emotional roller coaster these days? It's just another sign that those pregnancy hormones, which are signaling an extreme makeover in your body, are doing their job. Look to God for the strength to take the ups and downs with grace, and to find joy in the midst of the wild ride of pregnancy.

Points for Prayer and Praise

Praise God for the stunning strides your little one is already making in growth and development. Praise Him for how He is fearfully and wonderfully making your son or daughter.

Pray for your little one in the midst of rapid growth and development. And pray also that your son or daughter may one day grow in his or her knowledge of Jesus, bearing the fruit distinctive of those who are being conformed to His image.

As you experience exhaustion, pray for God's grace to make it through the things you need to do, for help from friends and family as you need it, and for the ability to give yourself the grace to rest and accept help.

Mommy's Memory Verse

How beautiful on the mountains are the feet of those who bring good news, who proclaim peace, who bring good tidings, who proclaim salvation.

Isaiah 52:7

Sharing the Good News

*How beautiful on the mountains are
the feet of those who bring good news,
who proclaim peace, who bring good
tidings, who proclaim salvation.*

ISAIAH 52:7

The night my husband and I told my parents that we were expecting our first child, we had tickets for all of us to see *Oklahoma*. Before we left, I made an insert to go into the playbill about a show coming in March called *A Baby Story*. The flyer listed that I'd be playing the part of "Mom," my husband, "Dad," and my parents, the "doting grand-parents." We got there early to stuff our announcement into playbills for my parents. I'll never forget their joy when they saw the spring lineup!

Sometimes it's difficult to decide the right time to share your preg-nancy news. But whenever you do, it's a joyous time. New life is on its way. And that's reason to celebrate. For most moms, it's difficult to contain the excitement. You have life-changing news and you're eager to shout it from the rooftops.

But honestly, that's exactly how we should feel every day as we carry in our hearts the joy of the gospel. The word *gospel* literally means "good news." And what better news could there be than that through Christ, our sins can be forgiven, our lives made new, and our access to God opened wide. Does your heart burst to share Christ? If not, ask God to renew the joy of your salvation and your eagerness to share His gospel.

A lot of moms spend time thinking about exactly the right way to tell the baby news to their spouse, friends, family, or employer. Many times a one-size-fits-all approach simply isn't best. Likewise, when we share the gospel, we should put thought into the best way to share with a particular friend or relative. Brainstorm in the space below about people in your life who need to hear the good news and how they'd receive the news best.

Lord, I love this analogy. It's true there is no "formula", or one right way to introduce people to you. Put people in my life path, on my mind and heart who need you, and then may your Holy spirit guide our conversation with their uniqueness in mind ♡.

How did you, or will you, share the news of your new baby with your friends and family?

I thought I would do it in a cute, clever, Pintristy way... but I couldn't wait, I just told them haha!

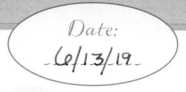

A Call to the Weary

"Come to me, all you who are weary and burdened, and I will give you rest."

MATTHEW 11:28

You may be sitting perfectly still right now, but your body is working at marathon levels. Your body is not only sustaining the development of a tiny little life but also essentially producing another organ—the placenta—to nourish and protect your child. On top of all that, your body now has to pump an extra amount of blood. By the time you reach your third trimester, your body will be pumping around 45 percent more blood than normal. That's a lot of strain on one body. It's no wonder you are exhausted.

Jesus does not chide or scold the weary and burdened. Instead He invites them to come to Him, to lean on Him, and to find rest in Him. While He cares about our bodies, which may be physically weary and longing for rest, He cares even more about our souls. He knows that the burdens we face in this world and the sins we wrestle to overcome all work together to make us weary and needy of spiritual rest and renewal. But He does not leave us to face our neediness alone. And He doesn't just sit back and wait for us to turn to Him. He actually *beckons* us to turn to Him and find the relief we so desperately need.

When you find yourself caught up in anxiety, in sin, or even in physical weariness, do you run to Christ? He is not your adversary, but your Strong Ally, your Comforter, and the One through whose strength you can overcome. Flee to Christ, dear one, and find rest.

Imagine for a moment that you are carrying a very heavy hiking backpack. Inside are all the things that are weighing you down: anxieties, sins, cares of this world, idols, regrets, bitterness, and more. Now unpack the bag and lay each item at the feet of Jesus. As you go through this mental exercise, journal about the things you're leaving with Him and the lightness you feel as a result.

I am laying down at your feet :
- Worry about my baby / development etc...
- finances
- Childcare situations
- My parents' situations
- Justin in his Job / safety / and being gone a lot.

Dear Little One,

In the early days of carrying you, I was often so tired that . . .

- one Sunday I slept until 1:00pm!
- Work was exhausting
- going on a jog was almost impossible because of how winded I would get!

Confirmation

By their fruit you will recognize them.

MATTHEW 7:16

*I*f you haven't already, you may visit your doctor or midwife some-time in the next few weeks for a confirmation of your pregnancy. While medical practices across the country vary quite a bit in terms of tests performed and even when they want to see patients, a nurse will likely ask you to give a urine sample and may or may not draw some blood. The office will use those samples to test whether you truly are pregnant (and if your appointment is closer to ten weeks, they may also check for such things as Rh factor and iron deficiencies). If you are pregnant, high HCG levels in your urine will confirm it. In fact, if you are pregnant, those HCG levels are doubling about every twenty-four to forty-eight hours. It's comforting to have a doctor confirm what you are likely already feeling to be true.

In the spiritual life Jesus also gives us a way to confirm the reality of our new life in Him. He tells us that if we are in Him, our lives will bear fruit. "Do people pick grapes from thornbushes, or figs from thistles? Likewise every good tree bears good fruit, but a bad tree bears bad fruit. A good tree cannot bear bad fruit, and a bad tree cannot bear good fruit" (Matthew 7:16–18). If you are a new creation in Christ Jesus, your life should be bearing fruit. You don't need to compare the fruit in your life to the fruit of others. That's not what this passage is saying. But it is telling us that there should be some evidence of the new life growing inside us.

God doesn't want us to be paranoid about our salvation, but He does encourage us to examine our hearts for the fruit of His work. Take a look back over the fruit of the Spirit in Galatians 5:22–23. List ways in which you have seen these grow in your life since you became a Christian.

Fruits: Love, Joy, Peace, Patience, Kindness, goodness, gentleness, & self-control. I see and feel evidence of each of these increasing in my life since Christ took over me. :-)

Fruit nourishes others. What is God planting in your life today that you hope your children will one day enjoy? Maybe it's the discipline of a daily time with God, or perhaps it's learning to control your tongue. Share it here.

- Spending time w/ Jesus as my best friend
- Selflessness
- "Soul Care"
- Thinking before speaking
- Living unoffended and quick to forgive.

Date:
6/15/19

The Nose Knows

*We are to God the aroma of Christ among
those who are being saved and those who
are perishing. To the one we are the smell
of death; to the other, the fragrance of life.*

2 CORINTHIANS 2:15–16

*T*here's nothing I love better than a good cup of coffee—that is, when I'm not pregnant.

My boss had come into my office to talk to me about an upcoming assignment, but the smell permeating from his coffee mug had me looking for an emergency exit. Surely he hadn't brought a cup of burning tar into my office? Maybe you've already begun to notice your changing sense of smell. Not only do all kinds of things smell stronger to you, but lots of smells you used to like smell perfectly repugnant to you now.

The apostle Paul used the metaphor of smell to describe how Christians will be received by those who do not know Christ. To the ones whom God is drawing to Himself, we are the aroma of life. To those who are perishing, we are the stench of death. In other words, sometimes a neighbor will respond to a simple statement of faith with anger or criticism that seems extreme. Yet other times a colleague will be drawn to us in ways that can only be credited to the supernatural power of Christ at work in us. Here's what we do know for sure: the response won't be neutral. The gospel offends or compels.

When it comes to sharing the gospel, we are only responsible to be faithful. We are not responsible for the results. How does that fact remove some of the pressure when it comes to sharing our faith?

That removes a ton of pressure! But it's also tough, because rejection is hard, and their is that risk... But Lord I pray that you give me boldness to get past that! and also to see that your gospel, life, and salvation is far more important that a potential "rejection". Make me loving, brave, & Bold!

Tell your little one about some of the changes you've noticed in how things smell or appeal to you now that you are pregnant. Have you noticed any cravings yet?

haha oh man, yes, definitely my sence of smell is heightened tremendously! and NO specific cravings... I'm just hungry all the time, and eat constantly! May you take in also those nutrients and grow healthy and strong little one! You're 8 wks-developed tomorrow! Keep going! you got this! God's got you! ♡

WEEK 8

The Wonder Within

About this time next year, your little one may be blowing raspberries (that cute sound babies make by putting their tongues between their lips and blowing air), but for now he or she is no bigger than one (0.63 in. and 0.04 oz.). But don't let the small size fool you. God's got a lot planned this week for your raspberry tart. Fingers and toes have begun to bud. Body and limbs may twitch spontaneously, but you won't feel movement for a while. And eyelids, nose, lips, and mouth continue developing into the face that will one day take your breath away. Neural pathways in the brain form as nerve cells spring to life. The heart has divided into two chambers and races at about twice the speed of your own.

Wonder is likely the last word you would choose to describe what's going on inside you this week—unless it is to wonder when the morning sickness will ever stop! For most women, morning sickness peaks around weeks ten and eleven, begins decreasing around week twelve, and disappears by week sixteen. For a smaller percentage of women it lingers until week twenty or may even persist throughout pregnancy. If you are part of the 50 percent of women who experience vomiting or the 70 percent who experience nausea, keep in mind that you are feeling ill because your body is doing exactly what it should be doing: sustaining God's formation of new life. If you are part of the minority who isn't sick, thank God, and when other pregnant women share the woes of morning-noon-and-night sickness, bless them by keeping your mouth shut!

Points for Prayer and Praise

- You may have had a doctor's visit to confirm your pregnancy by now. If so, praise God for the confirmation of this precious life.
- Pray for your little one's brain development this week and that he or she will one day worship God with heart, soul, and mind.
- Pray for the grace you need to get through the most difficult early symptoms of pregnancy: morning sickness, nausea, exhaustion, and aversions.

Mommy's Memory Verse

We do not lose heart. Though outwardly we are wasting away, yet inwardly we are being renewed day by day.

2 Corinthians 4:16

Be Still My Soul

*I have calmed and quieted my soul, like a
weaned child with his mother; like a weaned
child is my soul within me. O Israel, hope in
the LORD from this time forth and forever.*

PSALM 131:2–3 NKJV

I'll never forget the panic I felt when I was six weeks pregnant with
our second son and saw bright red blood staining my underwear. Was
I simply spotting (which is often a normal part of pregnancy) or was
I miscarrying? As the spotting continued over several days, my husband and I talked (sometimes through tears) about what our faith
should mean in such a time. We quieted our souls with the thought
that whether God took our little one home to Him or blessed us with
many years together, He was good, He was trustworthy, and He was
in control. Thankfully, we did not miscarry, but the lessons from that
scare stayed with us.

The picture in this psalm of a weaned child resting on his mother is
the picture of one who knows that his needs will be met, who knows the
heart of the One caring for him, and who can wait in faith. Our souls
are calmed and quieted when we remember God's promises—that He
works *all* things together for the good of those who love Him (Romans
8:28); that He will never leave us nor forsake us (Hebrews 13:5); and
that though others can be faithless, He cannot (2 Timothy 2:13). When
we look back and see His faithfulness, we are reminded that we can look
forward and trust His coming grace.

Even on our best days, anxious thoughts can plague our minds. What promises of God bring you comfort? Practice now stilling and quieting your soul by reflecting on these promises.

Lord, this devotion really came @ a perfect time. I know I can tend to err on the side of worry... and I'm sorry but it just feels like a fact, and it is (in this world, you will have trouble), and I don't like that, but then again who does! we all hate uncertainty... but you don't leave us there! You say (but take heart, for I have overcome the world!) Thank you for your promise that nothing could ever separate us from you... no matter how dark & despairing. Thank you also, for your promise to give us daily strength when we depend on you! Thank you for taking away so much of my anxiety as I have learned to depend on you, and to trust you ♥.

How does reflecting on God's faithfulness in the past give you hope in His future grace?

You have proven your faithfulness to me over and over again! Please remind me of those times when I feel hopeless... or out of control... also help me to be non-judgemental of people that are "doing wrong"... they are in your hands! Not mine! You give so much grace to me, now help me give it to others. Also even now, I pray against "mommy guilt", I do my best and forget the rest! Convict me if I not doing my best... but that's totally different!

Date: 6/21/19

Family History

If serving the LORD seems undesirable to
you, then choose for yourselves this day
whom you will serve. . . . But as for me
and my household, we will serve the LORD. ♡

JOSHUA 24:15

$\mathcal{W}$as it Great Aunt Matilda who had high blood pressure or Aunt Irene? You stare at the little boxes on the page in front of you in the doctor's waiting room, trying your best to check all that apply. It's the most morbid kind of survey there is: the family medical history questionnaire. While it's unpleasant to remember who in your extended family died or was plagued by illness, it's important information for your doctor to know in order to care for you and your baby.

Family history is also important when it comes to spiritual health. It can have a real bearing not only on your spiritual life but also on that of your child. Did criticism, backbiting, and arguments prevail in your home while you were growing up? Was sarcasm a way of life? ← yes Looking back, what unhealthy patterns of relating can you see? Or what positive head starts did you receive as a result of your parents' faithfulness? The good news is, God is bigger than the sins that have plagued our families even for generations past! And your generation has a decision to make: will you blindly repeat the unhealthy patterns of the past, or will you choose this day that your household will serve a better Master?

As you think about unhealthy patterns of relating in your family history, bring each of these issues to God in prayer. Ask God for the power to start new patterns and new traditions in your own household. What are some new and healthy spiritual habits you envision God helping you to pioneer in your home?

There was definitely sarcasm, but also Anxiety, depression, & self-esteem issues... Lord, again I ask you for the wisdom to lead a home that serves you, and puts you first. A home that trusts you Completely, & that is overflowing w/ your Joy! And who all know their identities as your children! Also show me how to cultivate a place of love + belonging.

Sometimes we get a head start in some area because of the faithfulness of a relative in our past. Tell your little one about a grandparent, aunt, uncle, or cousin whose legacy you hope will in some way shape him or her one day.

My Papa & Grammie (your great grandparents) have changed the trajectory of this family, for the better. They completely surrendered their lives to God, and they have been so invested in all of our lives so selflessly! They really love like Jesus, and serve like him too! They really embody the quote "If you want to change the world, go home & love your family." They also trust God so much through all the hard times they have endured. They really have an eternal perspective. ✒

Date: 6/22/19

Infinite Wisdom

*Oh, the depth of the riches of the wisdom and
knowledge of God! How unsearchable his
judgments, and his paths beyond tracing out!*

ROMANS 11:33

*A*s you think about your little raspberry-sized darling this week, consider how fast and furiously he or she has been growing since conception. In fact, your baby is already ten thousand times bigger since then! And guess what part is growing fastest of all this week? The brain. God is adding brain cells at a rate of about one hundred per minute. Sounds like you can safely go ahead and post that "My child is an honor student" bumper sticker on the back of your car.

While it's fascinating to consider the rapid growth of your little one's brain, it's even more awesome to consider the Mind that created not only your little one but also everything else that is knowable. When we stop and consider the mind of God, it is easy to get overwhelmed. How do you conceive of a Being that not only knows everything but also created everything? It's easy to get lost in wonder in just the mere knowledge of God, but when you add to that knowledge perfect wisdom, no wonder people break out in doxology. That is, after all, what the apostle Paul was doing in the passage above as he considered God's wisdom; he broke out in praise. How marvelous is the mind of our God!

Write a prayer of praise to God for His knowledge and wisdom.
What comfort does His perfect wisdom give you?

Lord, you are all-knowing, and all-powerful! Thank you for your Perfect wisdom! That only you have! It brings me so much comfort knowing that you are 100% good and 100% in control! And that you promise to share your wisdom w/ me when I ask for it! Help me to always trust in you and seek your wisdom ☺.

You may or may not consider yourself to be book-smart, but
everyone has an area of special knowledge or expertise. Tell your
little one something you've learned that's meaningful to you. If it's
something you're particularly passionate about, explain why you
love it so much.

Hi little bean, well I did pretty well in school ... but I would say certain areas that I shine and enjoy is with organization, which really helps w/ daddy's crazy schedule ... I guess God knew what he was doing putting us together ☺ I also enjoy reading & writing .. which is helpful in learning more about our wonderful God!

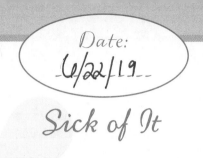

Sick of It

*We do not lose heart. Though outwardly
we are wasting away, yet inwardly
we are being renewed day by day.*

2 CORINTHIANS 4:16

*Y*ou may be in your first trimester of pregnancy if:

- you've spent so much time kneeling in front of the toilet,
  you've counted the floor tiles.
- you've wondered if it was a man who named it *morning
  sickness* because you would have called it morning-noon-and-
  night sickness.
- you would give just about anything for the woman in the
  cubicle next to you to stop eating leftovers at her desk. (Tuna
  casserole again? Really?)

The first trimester is in full swing, and what you wouldn't give to
feel good again!

While your situation is not as harsh in severity as what the apostle
Paul faced, his second letter to the Corinthians still has a worthwhile
application for you. You see, by the time Paul wrote his second letter
to the Corinthians, he had endured beatings, stoning, shipwreck—you
name it (2 Corinthians 11:25). But while outwardly he was a wreck,
inwardly he was vibrant. He commented how these "light and momen-
tary" afflictions will be as nothing when compared with the eternal

weight of glory (4:17). Like Paul, your body and spirit can move in two directions. Pray for the grace to be spiritually vibrant even while feeling physically ill. Ask God for His perspective. Ask for a glimpse of the glory your body will reveal at the end of these nine months and the even greater glory He will reveal at the end of time. Ask Him to show you that the joy will be more than worth the pain.

Where else in your life have you seen that the joy was worth the pain? What encouragement does meditating on this bring you?

- Working out and then feeling really good and getting healthy!
- Both me and Justin going through school then getting good paying jobs.
- humbling ourselves to live w/ Sandy & then get a house!

Write a prayer for your little one to have perseverance and perspective when he or she inevitably faces difficult times.

Lord, this is so timely, as this morning I prayed a prayer of strength, perseverance, and growing motivation over myself, so that I can truly experience Joy and live life to the fullest! I fervently pray this ability over my little bean as well! To trust you so wholeheartedly, to be a motivated, driven, problem solving, strong overcomer! Show me how to facilitate that growth wl'in them! which I know will be challenging because it will mean not always "rescuing" them, But yes may they have your perspective on life's situations & see things & people through your eyes. ♡

WEEK 9

The Wonder Within

The precious little life God is forming inside you is now about the size of a cherry (0.9 in. and 0.07 oz.). Through the wonders of ultrasound, doctors know that by this point in a typical gestation such small features such as the nose, lips, and ears have become more defined and identifiable (though still not in their final position on the head). The basic components of the eyes are now fully formed, and sometime this week the eyelids will fuse shut, not to reopen until about twenty-seven weeks. Gallbladder, pancreas, and sex organs begin forming this week (though they will not be distinguishable for several more weeks). And finally, the heart will finish dividing into four chambers.

Speaking of the heart, yours may skip a beat when you hear your baby's heartbeat for the first time. Your practitioner may use a Doppler device at your next checkup to take a listen. Don't worry if the practitioner can't find the heartbeat for another few weeks; sometimes women who carry a bit more weight or who have conditions like an anterior placenta (which simply refers to where the placenta attaches inside a woman) may find the sound muffled until the baby grows a bit larger. Also going on inside you this week: the placenta is now developed enough to take over hormone production. Those hormones have been causing the mood swings, nausea, and feelings of exhaustion you've been experiencing up till now, but rest in the fact that they are also signaling your body to do the important work of nurturing the life God is forming within you.

POINTS FOR PRAYER AND PRAISE

- Praise God if you've been able to see via early ultrasound the baby's heartbeat. (Note: Not all women will have an early ultrasound. Many practices will only do one at twenty weeks. Doppler listening devices are much more standard, however, and most practices begin using them between ten and twelve weeks.)

- As the four chambers of the heart are completed this week and the valves continue forming, pray for their physical formation to be without defect. Pray also that your little one's spiritual heart may always be soft toward God.

- Pray that you have the willpower to avoid any foods, drinks, chemicals, or toxins that will be dangerous for your baby and the discipline to eat healthy foods that will nourish you both.

MOMMY'S MEMORY VERSE

The LORD, He is the One who goes before you. He will be with you, He will not leave you nor forsake you; do not fear nor be dismayed.

DEUTERONOMY 31:8 NKJV

43

Sufficient Grace

*He said to me, "My grace is
sufficient for you, for my power
is made perfect in weakness."*

2 CORINTHIANS 12:9

$\mathcal{I}$n one of your upcoming visits, your health-care provider will likely ask whether you want to undergo certain screening tests to look for genetic or chromosomal abnormalities, such as Down syndrome, cystic fibrosis, or spina bifida. These tests run the gamut from harmless blood tests to a potentially life-threatening (for your baby) amniocentesis or chorionic villus sampling (CVS). Like so many things in pregnancy, you need to seek wisdom and weigh the potential risks versus potential gains.

It bears mentioning that as Christians we consider life to be sacred. As we choose whether to take tests like these, it should be with the intention of using this information only to be better prepared should we face the responsibility of caring for a child with special needs. It's also good to be aware that these tests may give mothers unnecessary reason for concern. According to the American Pregnancy Association, first- and second-trimester screenings will return a false positive about 5 percent of the time.

Whether or not you decide to be screened, it's a good time to reflect on how you would handle having a special-needs child. Remember the value that God places on each and every life. And reflect on His promise that His grace is sufficient for us in every circumstance.

Take time to pray about whether you will undergo optional screenings and at what point you will limit invasive tests should you get a concerning result. What does it mean to you to know that God's grace is sufficient for anything He allows in your life?

_____

_____

_____

_____

_____

_____

_____

In standard wedding vows, one promises to love in sickness and in health. Write a note to your little one, vowing your love for him or her in sickness and in health, for better and for worse.

_____

_____

_____

_____

_____

_____

Wisdom in Avoidance

Flee the evil desires of youth, and pursue righteousness, faith, love and peace, along with those who call on the Lord out of a pure heart. Don't have anything to do with foolish and stupid arguments, because you know they produce quarrels.

2 TIMOTHY 2:22–23

I was halfway around the globe for a speaking engagement and in the height of morning sickness. Finding something I could eat without getting sick was the trip's biggest challenge. Strong smells and strange tastes made an already nauseous mama sicker. And to make matters worse, there were regular servings of things I'd been told to avoid: cured and smoked deli meats, soft and unpasteurized cheeses, and wine.

When you are pregnant there are so many things you must avoid it can make your head swim. While some foods, drinks, and activities fall into gray areas, others are clearly unwise, even unsafe, to consume. It's better (and easier) just to stay away from them.

In the Christian life there are some things that are just better to avoid as well. Paul listed a few of them in his instructions to Timothy. Flee youthful lusts, and avoid foolish and ignorant disputes. Elsewhere in his letters Paul said to avoid divisive people (Romans 16:17), worldly wisdom (1 Corinthians 3:19), profane and idle talk (1 Timothy 6:20), and even the appearance of evil (1 Thessalonians 5:22). Sometimes wisdom isn't found in walking the line; it's found in walking away.

In the same way our personalities are different, our areas of struggle and temptation are different. Where we know we are weakest, avoidance may be key to standing firm in faith. Have you ever considered asking someone to hold you accountable in your areas of weakness? Why or why not?

_____

_____

_____

_____

_____

_____

_____

_____

Of the most common foods we are told to avoid during pregnancy, which will be hardest for you to go without?

_____

_____

_____

_____

_____

_____

Bounty Within the Boundaries

The boundary lines have fallen
for me in pleasant places; surely I
have a delightful inheritance.

PSALM 16:6

*W*hile food is the last thing you want to think about at this nausea-ridden state of pregnancy, filling your body with nutrient-rich foods is one of the best things you can do for your baby. Thankfully, the list of foods to pursue is much richer and longer than the list of foods to avoid. Whole grains, fruits, vegetables, calcium-rich foods, proteins, and healthy fats all top the list. And as an added bonus, pregnant women can enjoy guilt-free an extra 300 calories a day. Be careful not to focus so much on the must-not list that you miss out on the bounty of the must-have list.

Likewise, in your walk with Christ it's easy to get the mistaken notion that the Christian life is all about a set of thou-shalt-nots. If we have this view, we can get discouraged and easily tempted. Instead, the psalmist recognized the lushness of the pasture God had placed him in. He could rejoice in all the verdant space he had to roam and say with a full and glad heart that the boundary lines had fallen in pleasant places for him. Elsewhere, he spoke about his delight in the law (Psalm 119) because he understood that God's laws give the most bountiful life. When we see God as the Life-Giver rather than the Rule-Enforcer, our entire perspective shifts.

What wonderful things has God put within the boundary lines of your own life?

_____

_____

_____

_____

_____

_____

As a mother you will spend most of the days and years ahead training your little one where the boundary lines fall in his or her world. But if you see this job as simply rule-enforcer, you will miss out on the much greater role you have in showing your child that Christ is the Source of abundant life. Write out Philippians 4:8 here and pray over your role in teaching your child that which is good.

_____

_____

_____

_____

_____

_____

_____

49

Fear Not

The LORD himself goes before you
and will be with you; he will never
leave you nor forsake you. Do not
be afraid; do not be discouraged.

DEUTERONOMY 31:8

*M*y mom told me that with her first pregnancy she was paranoid that she would be the first person in history to crack under the pressure of labor and just not be able to deliver. Another friend confided that her biggest fear was losing her baby and having to explain it to her older sons. When it comes to pregnancy, anxieties—whether based in reality or in our imaginations—abound. Especially if this is your first time, there are so many unknowns. It's easy to let fear get the best of you.

But did you know that the most common command in the Bible is "Do not be afraid" (Deuteronomy 31:8)? Some scholars have calculated that this command is repeated 365 times. Maybe God knew we'd need to hear it every single day of the year! While we don't know all there is to expect while expecting, God knows every detail. He knows exactly how your pregnancy will unfold. And He promises that whatever comes, He will not leave you or forsake you. He will be with you through it all. What comfort there is in knowing that the Creator of the universe, the Wonderful Counselor, the Strong Deliverer, will be by your side every step of the way! Each time an anxious thought comes into your mind, take it captive. Pray about it and trust that God will give you the grace and the peace you need, no matter what comes.

Whatever anxieties are plaguing your heart today, take them before the Lord in prayer. What words of encouragement or comfort do you hear God speaking to you as you lay these requests before Him?

_____

_____

_____

_____

_____

_____

_____

Share a time in your life when God helped you be strong and courageous.

_____

_____

_____

_____

_____

_____

_____

WEEK 10

The Wonder Within

*T*his week God is still very much at work in the details of your little one's development. He or she is now approximately the length of a grape (1.2 in. and 0.14 oz.). Tooth buds are forming, small indentations on legs will soon be knees and ankles, arms are now able to bend at the elbows, tiny fingernails begin to appear, and a fuzzy covering of hair (called lanugo) begins covering the body for insulation. (Don't worry that your baby will be born looking like a miniature schnauzer, however; once your baby starts packing on the final pounds in utero, the lanugo will begin to disappear, having served its purpose.) Also this week: webbed hands and feet separate into individual digits when a masterfully synchronized signal cues the cells in between the digits to self-destruct, creating precious little fingers and toes. And if you have a boy, his testes are already beginning to produce testosterone.

During pregnancy many of your digestive functions slow down. God designed our bodies to do this in order to make sure Baby gets as much of the rich nutrient content from what we eat and drink as possible. The flip side, however, is that the slower digestive system, along with those prenatal vitamins you may be taking, may be causing your system to congest. You can combat the backup with high-fiber fruits and vegetables, which also have added nutritional benefits for you and Baby. Also, eat smaller, more frequent meals, which will make you feel fuller longer and keep your blood sugar from crashing.

POINTS FOR PRAYER AND PRAISE

- Praise God for good prenatal care. Most women throughout the world do not have such a luxury.
- Pray for the details of your baby's formation. Pray also that your little one will grow up knowing that God cares about every detail of his or her life.
- Pray for yourself, that as hormones take you on an emotional roller coaster, you will continue to treat all those around you in a way that pleases God.

MOMMY'S MEMORY VERSE

Be kind and compassionate to one another, forgiving each other, just as in Christ God forgave you.

EPHESIANS 4:32

Date:

No Angel

*Be kind and compassionate to one
another, forgiving each other, just
as in Christ God forgave you.*

Ephesians 4:32

*L*et's face it: you may be no angel to live with right now. Your mood swings may have you crying one minute and lashing out the next. The slightest smell can be offensive to you. And the sight of your husband's burrito has you practically bulldozing him down as you make a beeline for the bathroom. So much is happening inside you that it's difficult for husbands to take it all in, much less know how to sympathize properly. You are just as likely to be upset with him for saying you are finally starting to look pregnant as you are to be upset with him for saying you are not even looking pregnant yet. He can't win for losing.

If this describes you at all, or if you can't see how it could possibly describe you—I mean, you're a saint, after all, *and* the one suffering here—then it's probably a good idea to meditate awhile on Ephesians 4:32. Though you may be the one hugging the toilet, your husband is still in need of your kindness and compassion. And when he makes that remark that wounds your tender pregnant feelings, forgive as Christ forgave you. When you vowed to love one another in sickness and in health, you vowed to love him even while feeling sick, even while hormonal, and even while finicky. Live out that vow now through kindness, compassion, and forgiveness.

Write a note of appreciation for your husband. Read it to him tonight.

_____

_____

_____

_____

_____

_____

_____

Dear Little One,

I want you to know some of the qualities I admire most about your dad:

_____

_____

_____

_____

_____

_____

_____

_____

A Glorious Sound

I heard what sounded like a great multitude, like the roar of rushing waters and like loud peals of thunder, shouting: "Hallelujah! For our Lord God Almighty reigns. Let us rejoice and be glad and give him glory!"

REVELATION 19:6–7

Sometime soon your health-care provider will put a Doppler device to your belly and you will hear the unmistakable whoosh of Baby's heartbeat. It may be the most glorious sound you've ever heard: life—a little life—growing inside you! It is one of those milestones that may make your pregnancy suddenly feel real to you. After all, aside from a bit of bloating, you're probably not even showing.

As awesome a sound as that first heartbeat is, there's an even more glorious sound to come. The apostle John wrote about it in the book of Revelation. When time comes to an end and eternity dawns, we will hear a sound like a great multitude, like the roar of rushing waters, like loud peals of thunder, and then shouting. All the heavenly host will join together to say, "Hallelujah! For our Lord God Almighty reigns!" They will call us to worship, rejoice, be glad, and give Him glory. And what reason we will have to do so! For at that time, God will wipe every tear from our eyes, and we will dwell with Him forever. As you listen to that amazing sound of your baby's heartbeat, remember the sound of glory that is to come, and rejoice!

Imagine for a moment the end of all suffering, loneliness, deprivation, injustice, natural disaster, death, selfishness, hatred, prejudice, impurity, wickedness, and loss. This just scratches the surface of the blessing of our eternal hope. How does the hope of eternity spur you to live your life with hope and joy now?

_____

_____

_____

_____

_____

_____

_____

Describe what you felt the first time you heard your baby's heartbeat. (If you have yet to hear it, come back and fill in this section later.)

_____

_____

_____

_____

_____

_____

_____

Seek His Face

My heart says of you, "Seek his face!"
Your face, LORD, I will seek.

PSALM 27:8

Your little one is beginning to look more human and less alien this week. The ears are almost in their final shape, two sealed-shut eyes protect the tiny retina, the nose has a distinct tip, and tiny buds of teeth and taste buds are developing inside the mouth. It won't be long before you'll be stroking those soft cheeks, peering into those curious eyes, and watching those two lips blossom into first smiles. How wonderful it will be to see your baby face-to-face!

But as much as our hearts long to see our babies face-to-face, how much greater should be our longing for seeing the face of God. David cried out, "My heart says of you, 'Seek his face!' Your face, LORD, I will seek." In this psalm David wrote of his longing to dwell in the house of the Lord and to gaze upon the beauty of the Lord all his days. David was longing for relationship with God, for nearness to Him. His desire to see God's face was a desire to praise, adore, and emulate the very character of God and the radiance of His being. After Moses saw God's back, the people couldn't look directly at him because of his radiance. How much more would God's countenance shining upon us change us into dazzling reflections of His glory! Your face, oh Lord, we will seek!

What aspects of God's character fill your heart with longing for Him? List and describe these. Then take a few minutes to pray that you will come to reflect the radiance of His glory more and more in these characteristics.

_____

_____

_____

_____

_____

_____

_____

_____

Close your eyes and picture your future little one. Do you have any thoughts of what he or she will look like or whose likeness your baby will favor?

_____

_____

_____

_____

_____

_____

_____

Death Before Life

*"I tell you the truth, unless a kernel of wheat falls
to the ground and dies, it remains only a single
seed. But if it dies, it produces many seeds."*

JOHN 12:24

Your baby has been growing for almost a full trimester. But at this point in development, God has a very unusual event planned. Those webbed buds of fingers and toes are about to become separate digits, but in order for that to happen, something must die. At precisely the right time, the cells between fingers release a chemical message—a message of self-destruction. Similar messages control the formation of windpipes, brain, and stomach. In God's design, death seems to be a preprogrammed prerequisite to the formation of life.

It is no different in the spiritual life. Christ is very specific: unless we die to ourselves, there can be no true life. Discipleship cannot begin until we are ready to surrender all we have and are to God. Only then will He take us on the journey He has for us. Have you ever come to this point? If not, consider doing it now. You cannot hope to disciple this child whom God has entrusted to your care if you yourself are not willing to be a disciple—to relinquish all and follow Him. If you have already come to this place, are you seeing fruit? Spiritual death precedes spiritual life. A seed's death prepares the way for those tender shoots to sprout and, in good time, bear fruit.

Describe a time in your life when you let go of something only to see God bless you abundantly, more than you thought or imagined, through that very act of obedience.

_____

_____

_____

_____

_____

_____

Motherhood and sacrifice seem to go hand in hand. Make a list of some things in your life that will likely change when this new baby comes along. Conclude your list with this prayer: "Father God, I pray for the grace to sacrifice all that You ask of me with a spirit of joy, doing even the smallest things for my growing child as unto You."

_____

_____

_____

_____

_____

WEEK 11

The Wonder Within

The wonder of God's handiwork continues to be in the details this week, with minute changes making your little one—now the size of a lime (1.6 in. and 0.25 oz.)—continue to seem even less alien and more human. The ears are almost in their final place, and the tiny beds of fingernails and toenails develop. Arms and legs are now fully formed with hands, feet, fingers, toes, knees, and elbows that bend. And while it's still too early for you to feel noticeable movement, something more purposeful than mere twitching of the torso and limbs has begun. In fact, your baby is already beginning to try some somersaults and barrel rolls, getting ready for the next six months of gymnastic feats in the womb.

Your little one is not the only one growing. Your uterus is now about the size of an orange and has grown to fill your pelvis. The placenta continues to develop, and the umbilical cord now functions with its two arteries and a vein that will transport all of the food your baby needs. Speaking of food, if nausea has limited you from gaining weight so far, don't worry too much. The average weight gain during the first trimester is about 2 to 5 pounds, and there will be plenty of time for catching up if you've lost weight because of sickness. Do what you can each day to get the nutrients you need, and rest in the Lord.

POINTS FOR PRAYER AND PRAISE

- Praise God that all the major vital organs have by now been formed and are functioning. This means the risk of life-threatening defects decreases greatly this week.
- Pray for your little one as purposeful movement slowly develops. And pray that he or she may one day purposefully move toward God and not away from Him.
- Pray for the healthy development of the placenta and for your little one to get all the nourishment needed to thrive. Pray also that you might stay close to God, depending on Him for your spiritual nourishment.

MOMMY'S MEMORY VERSE

Let us draw near to God with a sincere heart in full assurance of faith. . . . Let us hold unswervingly to the hope we profess, for he who promised is faithful.

HEBREWS 10:22–23

Vital Connection

"I am the vine, you are the branches. He
who abides in Me, and I in him, bears much
fruit; for without Me you can do nothing."

JOHN 15:5 NKJV

One of the contributing factors of nausea in the first trimester is the hormones secreted by your developing placenta. While the weeks in which the placenta is forming can be rough for Mom, this spongy, pancake-shaped organ is a miracle in the making. It is made of exquisitely fine blood vessels interconnecting the chorionic villi, which are part of the border between maternal and fetal blood during pregnancy. These blood vessels, like roots of a tree, soak up all the necessary nutrients from a mother's blood and supply it to the developing baby via the umbilical cord. So efficient is the placenta that within two hours after eating, it will have passed along the nutrients from your food to your baby. The placenta and umbilical cord are literally your baby's life support.

Although we are not physically connected to God like a baby in utero, Jesus compared how desperately we need spiritual connection to a vine and its branches. How could the branches of a vine produce fruit—or live at all—if they weren't connected to the root? Our connection to God is so vital that Jesus said, "Apart from me you can do nothing" (John 15:5 NIV). Absolutely nothing. As you think about your little one growing inside of you, so dependent on you for his or her every need, remember how dependent you are on God. He sustains you and supplies the strength for every good work.

Read John 15:1–8. Take note of how many times Jesus commanded us to remain in Him. What practices help you "remain" in Christ? As you think about how your baby cannot yet survive outside the womb, remember that you cannot survive without God.

_____

_____

_____

_____

_____

_____

Once your baby is born, he or she will no longer be physically connected to you, but the dependence on you will still be great. In what ways are you looking forward to caring for your baby's needs? What ways of caring are you not looking forward to? Pray for the perspective to see this role as a privilege and not a burden.

_____

_____

_____

_____

_____

_____

Steadfast Love

*Because of the LORD's great love we are not
consumed, for his compassions never fail. They
are new every morning; great is your faithfulness.*

LAMENTATIONS 3:22–23

It's only been a few hours since you woke up, and already a television commercial made you cry, then tripping over your husband's computer bag made you lose your temper, and after that the sight of the booties your mom sent to congratulate you made you squeal with delight. If your life has been anything like this lately, it sounds like you have officially embarked on the pregnancy hormonal roller coaster.

Rising hormone levels are very real and very challenging to live with, but we are still responsible for how we treat those around us. It's not like we get a moral hall pass simply because our hormones are out of whack. When we do mess up (and let's be honest, chances are we are going to mess up more in these emotional days than we usually do), it's comforting to know amidst all our ups and downs that God does not change. He is the unchanging God: faithful, steadfast, immovable. And His covenantal love for us is not going to be undone by the ups and downs of our own faithfulness or emotions. His compassions never fail. As sure as the sun rises in the east, so we can count on the Lord our God faithfully forgiving us, loving us, and providing a safe place for us when we fail. The steadfast love of the Lord *never* ceases.

Isaiah 26:3 tells us, "You will keep in perfect peace him whose mind is steadfast, because he trusts in you." While our emotions can be all over the map, our minds can be unwavering as we meditate on the truths we know about God. Which truths of God do you need to reflect on in these emotional days?

_____

_____

_____

_____

_____

_____

_____

Write a note of love to your little one. In it, remind him or her of the even greater love of our steadfast God.

_____

_____

_____

_____

_____

The Hairs on Your Head

*"Indeed, the very hairs of your head are
all numbered. Don't be afraid; you are
worth more than many sparrows."*

LUKE 12:7

*W*ill your little one have curly locks of gold or the red-tousled strands that skip a generation in your family? Usually, in-utero hair development begins with eyebrows. And while hair follicles become apparent by this point in gestation, the actual hair won't push through and become recognizable until about twenty-two to twenty-five weeks. Even then it will not yet have pigment, so it's bright white. Not quite the picture you were imagining, huh?

Follicles of hair seem to form in a precise pattern. Spacing is perfectly equidistant. A whirling pattern will form on Baby's crown in utero and be influenced in its growth, configuration, and direction by the bulging growth of Baby's brain.

God is in every detail of your baby's development, orchestrating the growth of each hair. Not only does He know their number, He swirls their pattern, brings pigment to those strands, and foresees the exact moment when they will one day gray or fall out. God knows each one of us this intimately.

This kind of knowledge should give us confidence that God cares about *every* detail of our lives, no matter how small. Nothing happens outside His plan or His control. We are intimately known and fiercely valued by our heavenly Father—even to the very hairs on our heads.

Sometimes we may feel like the small things in our lives are not important to God. We may even neglect praying about matters that concern us because we think they just aren't big or weighty enough. After reflecting more deeply on today's passage, do you think anything is too small for God? What do you want to bring before Him?

_____

_____

_____

_____

_____

_____

_____

How will you seek to build intimate times of sharing and bonding with your child? Are there any special activities or traditions you want to develop that will help create such opportunities for closeness and heart-to-heart conversation?

_____

_____

_____

_____

_____

_____

Purposeful Movement

*Let us draw near to God with a sincere
heart in full assurance of faith. . . . Let us
hold unswervingly to the hope we profess,
for he who promised is faithful.*

HEBREWS 10:22–23

*W*hile it's still too early for you to feel any activity, your little one *is* moving. At first his or her movements are spontaneous twitches. But as millions of neurons develop each minute, they provide a neural network that creates coordinated movement. Gradually those movements and the muscular strength powering them become more purposeful and powerful. In the weeks to come, hands will open and close into tiny fists; knees, wrists, and elbows will bend; eyes will squint; lips will purse, open, and close. How miraculous to think about your son or daughter, hardly the size of a lime, already moving like this!

Though your little one's movements are currently more like reflexes, we have the advantage of purposeful, coordinated movements. And when it comes to our relationship with God, we can choose to move toward Him in purposeful pursuit, or we can choose to avoid Him in rebellious distance. We can open our hands and grasp the hope we profess, or we can bury our faces and live in a total despair that is unfitting for a child of God. Are you purposefully drawing near to God? James 4:8 promises us, "Come near to God and he will come near to you." What a promise! If only we would take advantage of it, moment by moment.

When you find yourself sinning, what is your first response? Are you more likely to avoid God in fear or run to Him for help? Pray for the grace to run toward God in failure. After all, He has the power you need to overcome.

_____

_____

_____

_____

_____

_____

Most of us have experienced times when God seemed incredibly close. Celtic Christians in the Middle Ages actually had a name for such times and places: they called them "thin places." Tell your little one about a thin place where God felt near to you.

_____

_____

_____

_____

_____

_____

WEEK 12

The Wonder Within

Your sweet little one is about the size of a clementine this week (2.1 in. and 0.49 oz.), still no bigger than your palm. Yet, masterfully, God is already at work developing reflexes in your darling clementine. A gentle nudge to the belly might make him or her wiggle out of the way. Fingers and toes curl, and facial muscles make reflexive sucking motions that will one day allow him or her to find sustenance. For now, however, the digestive system is practicing contractions while the intestines are still forming. Interestingly enough, the intestines have grown so fast that they are tumbling outside of the baby and into the umbilical cord. Soon, however, they will begin returning to their proper place—inside the abdominal cavity.

Meanwhile, your uterus is growing too big to fit neatly behind the pelvis and is starting to push its way into your abdominal region. That's why you may be noticing your clothes fitting a bit more snugly. That may be good news for you if you can't wait to buy a cute little maternity outfit to show off your soon-to-be-bulging belly. But if you're not so eager to abandon your current wardrobe, try the rubber band trick. Loop a rubber band through the buttonhole of your favorite pants and then back through the band itself. With the loop that's created, latch it around your pant button for a bit of extra give. Wear a longer shirt and no one will be the wiser! You can go a few more weeks without having to buy new maternity clothes or dip into the stash you put away after your last pregnancy.

POINTS FOR PRAYER AND PRAISE

- Praise God for the friends and family you've been able to share the good news with so far and for those who have truly rejoiced with you.
- Pray for your little one as he or she develops important reflexes for nourishment and protection. Pray that drawing near to God for spiritual nourishment and protection will also become reflexive for him or her.
- Pray for wisdom as you make decisions about whether to continue working outside the home or about any other adjustments that this new baby may require.

MOMMY'S MEMORY VERSE

If any of you lacks wisdom, let him ask of God, who gives to all liberally and without reproach, and it will be given to him.

JAMES 1:5 NKJV

What Starts Small

[Jesus] told [the multitude] another parable: "The kingdom of heaven is like a mustard seed. . . . Though it is the smallest of all your seeds, yet when it grows, it is the largest of garden plants and becomes a tree, so that the birds of the air come and perch in its branches."

MATTHEW 13:31–32

Since conception, cells have been multiplying at a dizzying rate. In fact, if your baby continued to grow at this rate after birth, he or she would be thirteen feet tall by one month. Yikes! Just eight weeks ago, your little one was the size of a poppy seed, about 1 millimeter. And now, although your little one is still small, the growth has been astronomical.

Jesus mentioned something else that begins small. He described the kingdom of heaven like a mustard seed growing from the tiniest of seeds to the biggest of garden plants. "The kingdom of God" is shorthand for God's eternal reign over all. In the New Testament it is inaugurated with Christ's coming (Matthew 2:2, Luke 16:16, John 18:37), but—despite the expectation of the Jews (and even many of the disciples)—Jesus explained that the worldwide reign of God would not come immediately in all its fullness. Christ inaugurated it, the church continues it (Matthew 24:14), and when Christ comes again, He will bring the kingdom in all its fullness (1 Corinthians 15:50–58). Talk about exponential growth!

The kingdom of God is certainly not easy to grasp in a quick study. We know that while God truly reigns over all now, there will still come a day when "every knee will bow" and "every tongue will confess" that Jesus Christ is Lord (Romans 14:11). How does that coming reality give you hope?

_____

_____

_____

_____

_____

_____

_____

One of the lies of the modern world is "It's all about me." The truth of the matter is, it's not. Your child will have to learn that life does not revolve around him or her; we revolve around God. Write a prayer for your child to come to understand this important truth.

_____

_____

_____

_____

_____

_____

Date:

- - - - - - - - -

Holy Adjustments

If any of you lacks wisdom, let him ask of God, who gives to all liberally and without reproach, and it will be given to him.

JAMES 1:5 NKJV

*E*ach baby brings with him or her a whole range of ways our lives must accommodate and bend. If you are a working mom, you are probably thinking a lot about your future work plans. Will you continue to work full-time outside of the home? Some moms may not have a choice in the matter. Others are able to work out flexible schedules to accommodate their growing families. Still others have the ability to stay at home for this special season in their lives. If you are already a stay-at-home mom, a new baby will affect some of the routines you've established and, most likely, some of the freedoms you've enjoyed as your other children have developed a bit more independence.

However it is that your life must bend and change in this new period, it's important that you seek God's wisdom for the direction you should go and His grace to accept these changes with a joyful heart. Seek the counsel of godly women who know you and your situation. And seek God's direction in prayer. He promises that if we seek His wisdom, He will freely give it to us. What better promise could we have than that the Lord of the universe stands ready and willing to counsel us in all our difficult decisions!

What difficult decisions are you facing as a result of this pregnancy? What are some of the factors involved? Spend some time bringing these needs before the Lord and asking Him to specifically guide you and give you wisdom.

_____

_____

_____

_____

_____

_____

_____

Tell your little one about one of the jobs you've had. What aspects of this job made your heart glad? (This question hearkens back to Proverbs 31:13, where a literal translation of the text would say that the wise woman works with "glad palms.")

_____

_____

_____

_____

_____

_____

A Snapshot in Time

This is the day the LORD has made;
let us rejoice and be glad in it.

PSALM 118:24

*H*ave you started taking pictures of that baby bump yet? If not, now's the time to start, before the baby bump gets away from you. You may not be so excited about your pregnant figure right now. But as time goes on, it's fun to look back and see a moment caught in time and the progression of your bulging belly.

While you are freezing that frame, it's a good reminder to stop and be present in the moment you're in. Pregnancy has a way of making us so forward-minded—after all, we're thinking about nursery colors, newborn nuzzles, and names—that we forget to be present and thankful in the now.

In Psalm 118 David captured the idea with a simple statement and command: "*This* is the day the Lord has made" (italics mine). Rejoice in *this* good day and be glad in it. No other day will be like it. Don't believe the lie that life is always around the next bend. Sure, there is much to look forward to with a baby on the way. But there is also something God has for you now, in this moment. He has work for you to do, joy for you to discover, and precious days for you to live on purpose. So live this day as if God gave it to you for a purpose—because He did!

What do you have to be thankful for today, right where you are? What is unique about this particular time in your life that may never come again? How can you take advantage of it?

_____

_____

_____

_____

_____

_____

Write a short snapshot of this moment in time for your little one. What is life like right now for Mom and Dad? What's going on today? Don't worry if the details are mundane; at some point your little one will enjoy getting a glimpse into an ordinary day in your lives before Baby.

_____

_____

_____

_____

_____

Shout It Out

You who bring good tidings to Zion, go up on a high mountain. You who bring good tidings to Jerusalem, lift up your voice with a shout, lift it up, do not be afraid; say to the towns of Judah, "Here is your God!"

ISAIAH 40:9

If you've kept the news that you're expecting a secret thus far, now is the time to go ahead and shout it from the mountaintops. As the first trimester closes, the risks of miscarriage—one of the main reasons people keep the news a secret—has dropped dramatically. So go ahead, call your friends and family, make a post on Facebook, tell the neighbors. You're having a baby!

In the book of Isaiah, the prophet foretold the coming salvation of Israel through the Messiah. While the Messiah had not yet come, God had assured Isaiah of the reality of this coming salvation. It was so certain that he could shout it from the mountaintops and tell it everywhere.

Being on the other side of the cross, we have the luxury of spreading the good news of Christ with a fuller picture of what that salvation means. The gospel is not simply good news; it is the *best* news. Christ has come. He lived a perfect life and carried the full weight of our sin to the cross, satisfying the wrath of a just God, that we might live at peace and know the fullness of life with Him. That's news worth shouting!

Could you clearly articulate the gospel message to someone who had no understanding of it? Practice here in the space below.

_____

_____

_____

_____

_____

_____

_____

Tell your little one about some of the reactions of your family and friends as they heard the news of his or her expected birth. Who shocked you with their enthusiasm? Who couldn't wait to lavish a gift on the little one?

_____

_____

_____

_____

_____

_____

WEEK 13

The Wonder Within

Your little one is about the size of a peach this week (2.9 in. and 0.81 oz.) and sporting a similar fuzziness as a fine coating of hair (called lanugo) now covers and insulates the body. By God's amazing design your peach is gaining more control over his or her movement, learning to make a fist and possibly sucking the thumb. (Where's the camera, right?) Also, this week the vocal cords and larynx begin developing, getting Baby ready for those coos that will melt your heart this time next year (along with those ear-piercing screams when your little angel is hungry or wet!). Intestines have moved back inside the body into their correct place. Meanwhile, bones in the arms and legs are beginning to form.

It's a gradual change, but little by little you may be noticing that you are spending less time feeling queasy. And walking by a restaurant may make you hungry instead of just wanting to run to the nearest toilet stall. If so, thank God for the relief! And here's another reason to thank Him: the risk of miscarriage decreases dramatically at this point in pregnancy. Add that to the fact that you're starting to show a little, and there's good reason that you'll soon be shouting the baby news from the rooftops if you haven't already. This is also the time many parents choose to share the news of the baby with their other children and prepare them for the arrival of the younger sibling. Talk about some good reasons to praise God!

Points for Prayer and Praise

🍼 Praise God for the time pregnancy provides you to prepare your heart, mind, and spirit for mothering this new little one.

🍼 Pray for your baby as bones begin forming, providing the scaffolding for the whole body. Pray also for the spiritual scaffolding of God's laws to one day strengthen and support him or her as a person.

🍼 Pray that as you share your news and as your conversations gravitate toward the new baby, you will be considerate and mindful of others who may be longing for children or may have suffered a miscarriage.

Mommy's Memory Verse

Remind people to . . . be ready to do whatever is good, . . . to be peaceable and considerate, and to show true humility toward all men.

Titus 3:1–2

Unsolicited Opportunities

I have become all things to all men so that
by all possible means I might save some.
I do all this for the sake of the gospel,
that I may share in its blessings.

1 CORINTHIANS 9:22–23

*N*ow that you've likely shared your news and may be starting to show, get ready for your share of unsolicited advice. You may even have perfect strangers chatting with you at the grocery store because so many mothers feel an instant bond with a pregnant woman. While you shouldn't have to deal with something that may be disturbing (I've changed the subject when I could tell someone was launching into a labor horror story), for the most part, getting advice, even the unsolicited kind, won't harm you. Just remember to keep your doctor as your primary source for information and as your sounding board.

As a Christian, don't look at all the advice as just a nuisance of pregnancy. See it as an opportunity. Paul said that he had become all things to all people for the sake of the gospel. He is talking here about finding common ground. But in these situations, people are already finding common ground with you. They are connecting with you and giving you an opportunity to connect back. So the next time a perfect stranger asks you your due date or your great aunt shares about life with a newborn, instead of tuning out, tune in. Say a silent prayer to use this chance to form a connection with someone for God's glory and for the sake of that person's eternal destiny.

Sometimes it's hard to welcome unsolicited advice as an opportunity for the gospel. After all, people may be insensitive, you may be busy, or you might honestly just rather be left alone. How are all of these scenarios actually opportunities to respond with a Christlike attitude?

_____

_____

_____

_____

_____

_____

_____

What advice have you already gotten from people? What has been good, what has been bad, and what has just made you laugh? Tell your little one about it.

_____

_____

_____

_____

_____

_____

_____

Keeping in Step

*Since we live by the Spirit, let us
keep in step with the Spirit.*

GALATIANS 5:25

*Y*our peach-sized wonder is trying something new this week. It's called the stepping reflex: as the feet touch something firm—in this case, the wall of the uterus—your baby reflexively responds in a stepping or kicking motion. Your pediatrician will likely check for this reflex after birth, but your little one is already clocking in the practice now, getting ready for a lifetime of steps ahead.

A reflex is by definition something we don't think about. It's involuntary. When it comes to our walk with God, there is both a reflexive and a volitional aspect to keeping in step with Him. If we are in Christ, we are a new creation. We are filled with His Spirit. As we walk in that relationship, our steps are characterized by the fruit of the Spirit (Galatians 5:22–23). We should grow more mature in these attributes and, to some degree, become able to reflect them reflexively. At other times, we must consciously make an effort to bring our steps into alignment with God. The psalmist wrote, "I have considered my ways and have turned my steps to your statutes" (Psalm 119:59). This describes a deliberate turning away from sin. We need to pray for the grace both to walk with God reflexively, out of our core being as new creations, and to walk with God volitionally when we face temptation or as we strive to grow more like Him.

Can you think of a time when you behaved in a godly way almost reflexively? Can you think of a time where you really had to willfully choose to walk according to God's commands? Describe both here and pray for the grace to keep walking in step with the Spirit.

_____

_____

_____

_____

_____

_____

_____

Write a prayer for your little one's physical development in the womb as he or she develops this stepping reflex. Also pray that his or her life will be marked by walking in step with God.

_____

_____

_____

_____

_____

_____

_____

A Voice to Praise

Let everything that has breath
praise the LORD. Praise the LORD.

PSALM 150:6

*I*n the past few weeks your little one has doubled in size. The digestive system is gearing up with practice contractions, getting ready for those sweet potatoes, bananas, and avocados you'll be spooning up by this time next year. Fingers are now not only separated into individual digits but also may be finding their way to Baby's mouth as he or she already practices thumb-sucking. And vocal cords are coming to completion this week, getting ready for that first solo in around twenty-seven weeks.

Baby awaits air to fill those lungs and let those vocal cords vibrate with a joyful noise. But you've got no reason to hold back. Whether or not you consider yourself a good singer, God loves to hear your voice raised in praise. In Psalm 150 David said, "Let *everything* that has breath praise the LORD" (italics mine). You are among that "everything," and God has given you more than enough reason to praise Him.

So what are you waiting for? Lift up your voice. What are some of God's acts or attributes that you want to praise? Chances are you know a hymn or praise song that can lead your heart to worship. Don't hold back; lift your song of praise today to the One who created your voice and who is now fashioning that new voice inside of you to sing His praises.

What is it about music that actually helps us draw closer to God? How do you worship God best through music? (Listening, singing, playing an instrument, etc.)

_____

_____

_____

_____

_____

_____

_____

Do you have an all-time favorite hymn or worship song? Tell your little one about it. How or why does it ignite your heart to praise God?

_____

_____

_____

_____

_____

_____

_____

Considerate Conversations

*Remind the people to . . . be ready
to do whatever is good, . . . to be
peaceable and considerate, and to
show true humility toward all men.*

TITUS 3:1–2

As you begin showing and sharing your news, there will be people in your life who struggle to rejoice with you or perhaps even be around you. Sometimes we know who those people are; sometimes we don't. Maybe an older sibling is still single and desperately longs to be married. Your news may make her feel like life is passing her by. Or maybe one of your good friends is struggling with infertility. It's not something she talks about, but there's a lump in her throat when she sees someone expecting. Or there may be a woman in your life who recently miscarried. You may be unaware of the pain in her heart as she congratulates you.

My point isn't that you should hide your news or even your joy, but rather, as the Bible urges us, be considerate and gentle toward everyone always (Titus 3:2). If you know someone who is struggling with this kind of issue, consider breaking the news privately or even in a letter. And when you feel like chatting about baby booties and nursery colors and names, seek out the women who are overjoyed to have discussions like these rather than the ones with whom each little comment feels like another dagger to the heart.

Are there people in your life with whom you need to be sensitive when sharing the baby news or talking about your excitement? How can you show consideration to them?

_____

_____

_____

_____

_____

_____

As you think about all the women who long for a child or marriage, it puts into perspective the blessing you are experiencing as you pat your growing belly. In light of this, write a prayer of thankfulness here for your baby and pray also for those you know who are struggling with unwanted singleness, infertility, or miscarriage.

_____

_____

_____

_____

_____

_____

Your Growing Wonder:
Second Trimester

WEEK 14

The Wonder Within

This week while walking the produce aisle, pick up an apple. That's about the size of your little one, stretching out to about 3.5 inches long (crown to rump) and weighing around 1.5 ounces. That little apple of yours is mastering some new skills this week: pursing the lips, frowning, and squinting. Don't you wish you had a womb with a view! Even though it will still be weeks before you feel your little kickboxer, his or her arms and legs are more active, and the movements have progressed from something like twitches to much more fluid motions. While the head has up to this point dwarfed the rest of the body, by the end of this week, arms and legs will have grown much more proportional.

What about you? As you enter your second trimester, you'll likely feel your energy returning. That's because, by the grace of God, most of the fetal organ development has taken place—but that's not to say there isn't a lot more maturing to do. Your uterus has been pushing just beyond your pubic bone for a couple of weeks now, which in turn means your pregnant belly may already be protruding. You may experience some discomfort as your uterus continues to grow and push aside your other organs. Isn't it marvelous, though, how God has designed a woman's body to make way for Baby?

Points for Prayer and Praise

- As you enter the second trimester, the risk of miscarriage drops dramatically. Praise God for the healthy development of Baby so far.
- Pray for the maturation of key organs this week, such as your baby's spleen (producing red blood cells now) and intestines (now producing meconium).
- Pray for self-control and healthy decision making as nausea decreases and food begins to sound good again in the next few weeks.

Mommy's Memory Verse

The grace of God that brings salvation has appeared to all men. It teaches us to say "No" to ungodliness and worldly passions, and to live self-controlled, upright and godly lives in this present age.

Titus 2:11–12

Green Pastures

*He makes me lie down in green
pastures, he leads me beside quiet
waters, he restores my soul.*

PSALM 23:2–3

*C*ongratulations on reaching your second trimester! Doesn't it feel great to know that the most difficult days of morning sickness are likely in the rearview mirror now? Many regard the second trimester as the best season of a woman's expectant journey. While your morning sickness may still be lingering, it should soon be gone. Your appetite starts coming back; your energy begins to return; your belly starts to show; and your discomfort is minimal. These are truly precious days worth seizing and enjoying!

God is so good to allow life's hard seasons—the valleys—to be tempered with seasons of green pastures and quiet waters. The hardest part for us is walking as closely with God in times of ease as we do in times of hardship. In the valleys, we pray desperately. But in the verdant pastures, we tend to forget Him and think we have earned the goodness happening to us. God warned the Israelites of this. He said, "When the LORD your God brings you into the land he swore to your fathers . . . filled with all kinds of good things you did not provide, . . . be careful that you do not forget the LORD" (Deuteronomy 6:10–12). So how do we stay mindful of Him? Offer God continual prayers of thanksgiving—whether you're in the valley *or* on the mountaintop. Doing so will remind you that the blessings you enjoy are not a matter of your own merit, but are all because of His grace.

As you look back on the first trimester, how has God ministered to you in the valleys? What have you learned about Him in this time?

_____

_____

_____

_____

_____

_____

_____

What do you have for which you are thankful, especially as you consider the first trimester coming to a close and the second beginning?

_____

_____

_____

_____

_____

_____

_____

_____

The Fingerprints of God

We have different gifts, according
to the grace given us.

ROMANS 12:6

You know, not even identical twins are identical. One way in which they are different is actually going on with your baby this week: fingerprint formation. While the overall ridge and valley structure of fingerprints have a genetic factor, the density and position of the amniotic fluid in the womb actually affects the curves and ridges of the fingerprints creating those utterly unique patterns in utero. As your baby moves his fingers through the fluid, the particular, detailed patterns are formed. Amazing, isn't it?

It's not just fingerprints that make us each so thoroughly unique. For His own glory God gives us different personalities, different gifts, and different callings. His absolute creativity and His vastness are reflected in the uniqueness of His creations. As we fully allow our personalities and gifts to be redeemed, developed, and used, we bring God glory in the greatest of ways. That's because in doing so we reflect another aspect of His complexity, diversity, and creativity as no other person has or ever will—because there's only one *you*. And when our gifts are being used, we are complementing one another not just for the purpose of doing good works, but also for the purpose of illuminating the bigger picture the world sees of who God is—a magnificent and vast Creator.

Think for a moment about the infinite and absolute creativity of God in making us all so different. How does this lead you to praise Him?

_____

_____

_____

_____

_____

_____

_____

Write a prayer for your baby, that he or she will one day fully discover the unique talents God has given him or her. Pray that your little one may use and express these fully, not for his or her own glory, but for God's and for the good of His kingdom.

_____

_____

_____

_____

_____

_____

_____

The Glow

They looked to Him and were radiant,
and their faces were not ashamed.

PSALM 34:5 NKJV

You may have had someone tell you that you have that pregnancy "glow" about you. Or maybe you are still green with morning sickness. But interestingly enough the pregnancy glow isn't just another old wives' tale of pregnancy. There is actually a biological basis for it. During pregnancy there is an increased blood flow, and that extra volume of blood causes the cheeks to look flushed. It's similar to the way you might look after extra exertion or excitement. Additionally, your skin glands are producing extra oil, which may give your face a certain sheen. And you thought people were just being nice when they told you that you were glowing!

The Scriptures also talk of a glow that believers of Christ should have. In Psalm 34 David said that those who look to God are "radiant." And in 2 Corinthians 3:18 Paul referenced Moses having to wear a veil because of how his face shone with radiance after seeing God's back. Paul contrasted how, on this side of the Cross, "we, who with unveiled faces all reflect the Lord's glory, are being transformed into his likeness with ever-increasing glory, which comes from the Lord, who is the Spirit." What did both David and Paul point to as the reason for our radiance? Apparently, the secret lies in looking to or contemplating Christ. We shine with His radiance as we are transformed into the image of God.

Brides are often called radiant. How do the joy and happiness of a woman reflect the good character of the bridegroom? Does your countenance reflect the goodness of Jesus, your eternal Bridegroom? Contemplate His goodness.

_____

_____

_____

_____

_____

_____

Dear Little One,

Some people call it a glow. I call it love. My heart is full of so much love for you and it can't help but come out on the outside. I want you to know that before I ever held you, I loved you. I want you to know . . .

_____

_____

_____

_____

_____

_____

Satisfied in God

*The grace of God that brings salvation
has appeared to all men. It teaches us
to say "No" to ungodliness and worldly
passions, and to live self-controlled, upright
and godly lives in this present age.*

TITUS 2:11–12

*T*here finally does come a day when, out of nowhere, the thought of food doesn't make your stomach turn—food actually starts smelling and tasting good again. You have an appetite, and it feels so good to feel good. If you've arrived at this point, congratulations! If you're still waiting, hang in there. For all but a small minority, morning sickness disappears by around sixteen weeks.

But once food starts tasting good again, watch out! You'll be amazed how easy it is to pack on the pounds. The expression "eating for two" can be somewhat deceiving when one of you is only about the size of an apple. Adding about 300 calories a day is not the license for the all-you-can-eat dessert buffet you were dreaming about. And while pregnancy is definitely no time for dieting, it is also no time to fill your body with junk. Self-control is still the name of the game.

Likewise, the book of Titus tells us that the grace of God teaches us to live self-controlled lives. How is that? When a heart is truly satisfied in God, it doesn't have to look to other things to give it satisfaction. A heart that is satisfied in God finds pleasure in Him rather than polishing off the entire carton of Häagen-Dazs.

How would you evaluate your level of self-control, not just in the area of food, but in all areas of your life? We're mistaken if we think self-control is merely a matter of the will; it's a matter of the heart. Pray for the grace to find your satisfaction more wholly in God and thus to be able to say no to all kinds of ungodliness.

_____

_____

_____

_____

_____

_____

_____

In what ways is good self-control vital to good parenting?

_____

_____

_____

_____

_____

_____

_____

WEEK 15

The Wonder Within

*W*ith many of the challenges of the first trimester coming to a close, you are likely breathing easier; meanwhile your little one is just taking his or her first practice "breaths." At this point breathing consists of moving amniotic fluid in and out of the nose and upper respiratory tract. It's good practice for when he or she takes those first *real* breaths in about six months. In addition to doing new breathing exercises, your little one is now about the size of a navel orange (4 in. and 2.5 oz.), with legs growing longer than arms, and joints and limbs all flexing and moving. Because your baby still hasn't begun packing on the pounds, the skin is still thin and translucent. That will change soon, however, as baby continues to plump up in the weeks to come.

If you're a first-time mom, you likely won't feel any fetal movement until around eighteen to twenty weeks. But if you've been pregnant before, you may be in tune enough with what you're feeling to recognize the first early movements of your little wonder. If not, no need for concern. It's still very early in Baby's development. In terms of your development, on average a woman has gained around 5 pounds by this point in pregnancy. If morning sickness has your numbers down, talk to your health-care provider, but likely all is well and you'll be gaining weight in no time. If your weight has already skyrocketed, work on pacing yourself. A slow and steady weight gain is healthiest for you and Baby. Most health-care providers advise a total weight gain of 25 to 35 pounds for the average woman.

Points for Prayer and Praise

🍼 If you've begun to notice morning sickness lessening or energy returning, praise God for the relief. If you are still suffering with these symptoms, pray for strength and perseverance.

🍼 Pray for your little one as he or she practices breathing by moving amniotic fluid in and out of the mouth. Pray that one day your son or daughter will use the breath and voice given to him or her to praise God.

🍼 Pray that as you prepare to parent this new little one, you might seek out the friendship of wise women who can help you on the journey.

Mommy's Memory Verse

Whatever you have learned or received or heard from me, or seen in me—put it into practice. And the God of peace will be with you.

PHILIPPIANS 4:9

The Company We Keep

*Do not be misled: "Bad company
corrupts good character."*

1 CORINTHIANS 15:33

The way in which God nourishes your child in utero is amazing. Masterfully, the placenta transports food, water, and oxygen to your little one. In some places, its membrane is quite thin, about one cell thick. That's one reason expectant mothers must be so careful about what they put in their bodies. One cell may be all that separates your little one from what you put in your body. No wonder concerns about certain medicines, listeria, and alcohol are so very real. It also illuminates why it's important to eat and drink healthy, nutrient-rich fare. When we eat or drink, Baby does too.

The permeability of the placental membrane works the other way too. Some researchers believe that because some fetal cells pass through the placenta back into the mother's body, this may account for the reason women who have been pregnant tend to live longer and have reduced incidences of breast cancer, multiple sclerosis, and other illnesses.

Environment matters. And the same holds true in our lives as well. When we surround ourselves with negative people or bad influences, we are likely to internalize some of that sin and negativity. But putting ourselves in the midst of godly people, sound doctrine, and spiritual encouragement gives us the greatest chance for increasing our spiritual health. As mindful as you are about what you put into your body during this time, be mindful also of the people with whom you surround yourself.

Proverbs 12:26 says, "The righteous should choose *his friends carefully" (NKJV). Notice the word* choose. *Do you choose friends who inspire your love for Christ? Ask God if there are any godly women with whom He wants you to pursue a deeper friendship.*

_____

_____

_____

_____

_____

_____

_____

Tell your little one about some of the wise and godly people who have influenced you to be the woman you are today.

_____

_____

_____

_____

_____

_____

_____

Let It Show

If anyone says, "I love God," yet hates his brother, he is a liar. For anyone who does not love his brother, whom he has seen, cannot love God, whom he has not seen.

1 JOHN 4:20

Are you showing yet? Depending on your body type and whether you are a first-time mom, you may show early or late, but all pregnant mamas show eventually. The reality of what's going on inside you will one day cause outward change.

The same is true in the Christian life. The reality of our new birth in Christ will manifest itself on the outside. If our faith is real, there will be external proof, visible evidence of a heart transformed. Jesus told His disciples, "By this all men will know that you are my disciples, if you love one another" (John 13:35).

So here's the question: Are you showing yet? Is the reality of your walk with Christ evident to outsiders? In his first letter, John put it quite bluntly: you're a liar if you claim to love God yet hate your brother and sister. In Matthew 5:47 Jesus said that even unbelievers love those who love them, but Christians are called to love the hard-to-love. Wherever you find hate in your heart for another of God's image-bearers, repent and ask Christ to change you. If you are a follower of Christ, ask God to let it show by how you love.

What are ways in which your love for others is evident to those outside the faith? How does love affect our speech, our interactions, our attitudes, our time, and even our body language?

_____

_____

_____

_____

_____

_____

_____

Has anyone noticed you are pregnant yet? Do you feel like you're showing yet? Tell your precious baby about it.

_____

_____

_____

_____

_____

_____

_____

In Plain Sight

*Nothing in all creation is hidden from
God's sight. Everything is uncovered
and laid bare before the eyes of him
to whom we must give account.*

HEBREWS 4:13

*T*o find out or not to find out . . . that is the question. Soon, you'll
have the opportunity to get a sneak peek at your baby's development
in the womb, including the gender. If you and your husband are trying to decide whether you want to know before delivery, you'll need
to consider your feelings about being surprised. It's certainly easier
to pick out baby clothes and narrow down the name list when you
know the gender before birth. But there are fun aspects of waiting and
finding out on labor day. Having done it both ways, my husband and
I have experienced both the joy of the full wait and the extra bonding
of knowing ahead of time.

But while you are busy talking it over, God already has full
knowledge of your little one. Nothing is hidden from His sight. Not
only does He know your little one's gender, He knows the man or
woman he or she will become. The Alpha and the Omega knows your
child's beginning and end and all the days in between. Nothing surprises Him.

Theologians call this aspect of God His omniscience: He is all-
knowing, and it is one of the most comforting doctrines we have.
Nothing befalls us that shocks God. Not only has He seen everything

that will come our way, but He also works all things together for good for His children.

How is God's complete and total knowledge about your baby comforting? What assurance does it give you?

_____

_____

_____

_____

_____

_____

Which way are you leaning: to find out or not to find out? What are the important factors for you and your husband?

_____

_____

_____

_____

_____

_____

_____

Practice

Whatever you have learned or
received or heard from me, or seen
in me—put it into practice. And
the God of peace will be with you.

PHILIPPIANS 4:9

Your baby has already acquired quite a few skills by this point in your pregnancy. Around nine weeks Baby started sucking practice and by now can put those tiny little fingers to the mouth. Around thirteen weeks Baby started breathing practice. Obviously he or she is surrounded by fluid in the womb, so this isn't breathing like you or I do it. But he or she is moving amniotic fluid through the mouth and nose, priming for life outside. And finally, baby is also practicing that stepping reflex, when little feet bump up against the solid walls of your uterus. Soon, in fact, you may begin feeling tiny flutters.

All of us must practice in order to improve our skills, whether it's running, writing, or piano playing. Even in the spiritual life, our spiritual muscles require flexing. Do you have a short fuse when it comes to slow traffic? Do you feel awkward in your conversations with God? Do you clam up when it's time to share your testimony? Or is it hard for you to be quiet and truly listen to the hearts of others? Whatever your areas of struggle, ask God for His empowerment as He presents opportunities to improve. Then give yourself grace to flail, to keep trying, and to do a little bit better each time.

In what areas of your spiritual life do you usually work in your own strength and then get frustrated? Pray now for God to empower you to relinquish your will to His. And then be bold enough to ask God for some opportunities to practice.

_____

_____

_____

_____

_____

The second trimester for Baby is all about practice. But in many ways the first few years with Baby are all about practice too. They practice eating, walking, talking, going potty, and dressing. As exciting as these new steps are, moms need lots of patience as little ones spew peas, throw tantrums, and piddle in corners. Write a prayer for your own patience and for grace toward yourself and your little one in the days and months ahead.

_____

_____

_____

_____

_____

WEEK 16

The Wonder Within

With every day that passes, God is helping your little one gain new strength, skills, and vitality. From hardly the size of a poppy seed, he or she has grown to about the size of an avocado (4.6 in. and 3.5 oz.), capable of filling your cupped palm and filling your heart to overflowing. Already, your little one's ears and now eyes are in their final position on the head. The developing facial muscles are making it possible for your little wonder to smile, squint, or grimace while the developing back muscles help your baby pull his or her head up out of the characteristic fetal curved position. In the weeks ahead he or she will double in weight.

You're likely beginning to gain some weight yourself, and at least some of it is due to the sustaining network that houses your little one. Your uterus now weighs about 8.5 ounces, and the top can be found about halfway between your pubic bone and navel. Additionally, you are carrying about 7.5 ounces of amniotic fluid and about 50 percent more blood in your body. All that extra blood may be contributing to what some people call "the glow" of pregnancy, making you look a bit flushed. Of course, hormones may also be contributing to some acne. However your looks are changing, remember there's a miracle growing within you, and let that thought fill you with the glow all of us can have as Christians: joy.

Points for Prayer and Praise

- Praise God for how He has designed your body to nourish and protect this little life.
- Pray for your little one's developing muscles. Pray also that he or she will develop spiritual fortitude for resisting temptation and holding steadfast to the Lord.
- Pray that you will make healthy choices both in what you eat and in your physical activity level.

Mommy's Memory Verse

As God's chosen people, holy and dearly loved, clothe yourselves with compassion, kindness, humility, gentleness and patience.

Colossians 3:12

A Stirring

*"The wind blows wherever it pleases. You
hear its sound, but you cannot tell where
it comes from or where it is going. So it
is with everyone born of the Spirit."*

JOHN 3:8

I vividly remember the first times I felt my babies move. With my oldest, it was at a Navy-Air Force football game. With the baby I'm carrying now, it was after eating some chocolate cake for our wedding anniversary. Some women describe those first movements like popcorn popping, butterflies fluttering, or goldfish swimming. If you are a first-time mom, you may have to wait a few more weeks, but if you are a veteran, it's likely you've already begun feeling movement.

It's undoubtedly one of the strangest and most wondrous things about pregnancy, feeling a little life moving within. The wonder of those little flutters (and later karate chops) is something that never gets old.

In some ways the movement of the Spirit of God is similar. Jesus likened the Spirit's movement to the wind: we can see the wind's effects, but we can't see the wind and we definitely can't control it. Likewise, we can feel our babies, but we can't see them. And as any mama who's had Baby keep her up late can tell you, we can't control when that movement starts and stops. Seeing the Spirit move in our lives, like feeling our babies move, is one of those wonders that should never get old. Let them both nudge you to praise.

Just as I can vividly remember the first time I felt my baby move, I remember the first time I felt the Spirit of God at work inside me. If you can remember such a time, what was it like? If you can't, write about some evidence you've seen of the Spirit's work in your life.

_____

_____

_____

_____

_____

_____

Have you begun to feel the baby move? If so, describe it. Where were you when you first felt it happen? If not, come back and fill in this section when you do. Note the date you first felt movement.

_____

_____

_____

_____

_____

_____

_____

Clothed in Christ

As God's chosen people, holy and dearly
loved, clothe yourselves with compassion,
kindness, humility, gentleness and patience.

COLOSSIANS 3:12

You've likely packed the skinny jeans away for a while and now, much to your dismay, the baggy ones are getting impossible to button too. If this is your first baby, you may be able to get by for a little longer without switching to maternity clothes. But if this isn't your first go-around, it's likely you are already dipping into your maternity stash.

Whether you're shopping for new clothes, stalking consignment sales, or raiding your girlfriend's closet, putting on those maternity clothes is one way that helps the pregnancy journey begin to feel more real. Finally, all that's been going on inside you is becoming evident on the outside.

As God's people, we also get a new wardrobe. We are clothed in Christ's righteousness: His compassion, kindness, humility, gentleness, and patience. Through this the new creation inside is evident to the world outside. When our hearts overflow in mercy and sympathy, the needy see the heart of God. When we do good to another and do not expect anything in return, the hardened are softened. When we serve rather than wait to be served, the lowly are lifted up. Through our soft answers and sensitive treatment of people, the bruised see God's tenderness. And by our willingness to wait, we allow space for God to show up and work in the gaps. This is the fashion statement the world needs most.

Why do you think the qualities mentioned in Colossians 3:12 are especially important for mothers to evidence to their children? How will these qualities help our little ones grow up to know God?

_____

_____

_____

_____

_____

_____

_____

Have you bought or borrowed any maternity clothes yet? Tell your little one about it.

_____

_____

_____

_____

_____

_____

_____

_____

Worth the Cost

*[The ant] has no commander, no overseer
or ruler, yet it stores its provisions in
summer and gathers its food at harvest.*

PROVERBS 6:7–8

*M*aybe you're still floating on air from finding out the news that you are expecting. Or maybe you've been fretting about finances since you first saw your plus sign. Whether you're a head-in-the-clouds kind of mama or a fearful one, God doesn't want you to stay in either place when it comes to the issue of financially preparing for your future family.

Jesus told His disciples that even in ordinary matters, a wise man counts the cost (Luke 14:28–30). We shouldn't be ignorant about the realities of growing expenses. For instance, ask your insurance company what you can expect to pay for remaining doctor's visits and birth. But while Jesus encouraged us to consider the cost, He didn't want us to be afraid. He told us not to worry about tomorrow, but rather to look at the birds of the air and the lilies of the field and see how He cares for them (Matthew 6:25–30). We should be at peace, knowing that God will help us do what He has called us to do: raise a child. As we look squarely at the realities and trust God in them, we also follow the wisdom put out for us in the book of Proverbs. We consider the ant that stores away and learn there is wisdom in saving what we can today for the needs of tomorrow.

When it comes to finances, are you more likely to bury your head in the sand or give yourself an ulcer? Which of today's Scripture passages do you need to spend time meditating on further? Write out one of the following verses that you feel led to spend time meditating on or even memorizing: Luke 14:28–30, Matthew 6:25–34, Proverbs 6:6–18.

_____

_____

_____

_____

_____

_____

Write a short love note to your little one. Tell him or her that any sacrifices you make on his or her behalf will be worth the cost.

_____

_____

_____

_____

_____

_____

Exercising Godliness

*Bodily exercise profits a little, but godliness is
profitable for all things, having promise of the
life that now is and of that which is to come.*

1 TIMOTHY 4:8 NKJV

It's probably the last thing you feel like doing, yet physical exercise can help you beat pregnancy fatigue. And studies show that women who have maintained a moderate level of physical activity throughout pregnancy have easier labors and easier experiences taking the weight off postpartum. Consult your doctor before starting a new routine and use common sense. (Don't sign up for kickboxing!) A good rule of thumb is that you should be able to carry on a conversation while doing a cardiovascular exercise.

The Bible doesn't discount the importance of exercise. In fact, we are reminded that our bodies are temples of God and deserve the utmost respect (1 Corinthians 6:19). But while the apostle Paul taught that physical training has value, he also pointed out that the value of godliness far outweighs it. In fact, Paul exhorted Timothy to "train [himself] to be godly" (1 Timothy 4:7). How does that happen? As we pray for grace and rely on the Spirit, we must *exercise* self-control, kindness, gentleness, and all the other fruit of the Spirit (Galatians 5:22–23). That may mean practicing giving a word of encouragement when we'd rather be critical, or turning in early on Saturday night so we can fully focus as we worship on Sunday. As we rely on the Spirit and exercise our spiritual muscles, we grow in godliness.

List the fruit of the Spirit (Galatians 5:22–23). In which of these do you feel weakest? Pray for God's grace to grow in these areas and for opportunities to exercise these spiritual muscles.

_____

_____

_____

_____

_____

_____

_____

You've just listed the fruit of the Spirit. Take a few minutes to write a prayer for your little one to know God and abound in these fruits one day.

_____

_____

_____

_____

_____

_____

_____

WEEK 17

The Wonder Within

*Y*our little wonder may be making his or her presence known this week. Those arms and legs now are big and strong enough for you to feel movement. After all, he or she—about the size of a large sweet onion (5.1 in. and 5.9 oz.)—is not so little these days. And probably like you, he or she is starting to accumulate a bit of body fat by now. Baby is also becoming more substantial in bone mass as the skeleton changes from soft cartilage to bone in a process known as ossification. Meanwhile, the brain and central nervous system are coming to regulate more of your baby's body functions, including the beating of the heart.

As for you, the top of your uterus is now only about 2 inches from your belly button. And as your body changes, you may detect your center of gravity changing also. Watch out for falls and tumbles. You may also notice that you feel light-headed if you get up too quickly, so take it slow when rising. If you haven't already, you'll want to begin sleeping on your side, particularly the left side, which is the position that allows the best circulation for you and for Baby. Consider investing in a body pillow or using pillows you already have and putting them between your arms and legs. Doing this helps keep your hips in alignment as well as keep you comfy—or as comfy as one can be with a growing belly!

POINTS FOR PRAYER AND PRAISE

If you've begun to feel your little one move, praise God. Isn't it amazing to feel a little life alive inside of you? If you haven't yet, don't worry. You will likely feel movement within the next three weeks.

Pray for the development of your little one's bones. While you are praying that his or her bones may grow hard, ask God to keep his or her spiritual heart soft toward the things of God.

Pray for God to help you strengthen and improve the key relationships that will be important in your little one's life: with you, your husband, your parents, and your in-laws, for starters.

MOMMY'S MEMORY VERSE

"The Lord does not look at the things man looks at. Man looks at the outward appearance, but the Lord looks at the heart."

1 SAMUEL 16:7

Relationship Tune-Up

*Children's children are a crown to the aged,
and parents are the pride of their children.*

PROVERBS 17:6

*W*henever we are getting ready to go on a long trip, I always get a quick tune-up on the car. I know there will be a lot of strain on the vehicle crossing all those miles, and it seems like the least I can do is give her an oil change. It's a lot easier to do some preemptive maintenance than spend hours—perhaps even nights—stranded mid-journey when those worn-down tires blow or smoke begins pouring out of the engine.

As you prepare for Baby, you can anticipate putting a lot of miles of wear and tear on certain relationships. Could your marriage use a quick tune-up? What about those relationships with your in-laws? Do they need a little oiling to run smoother? You get the idea. Most of the time we already have an idea about the areas where things aren't running smoothly. Maybe there's an issue of unforgiveness with your parents or a lack of communication in some area with your spouse. The weak areas will get even more strained over the miles.

Grandparents have the right to a relationship with their grand-children. Children need parents they can be proud of. Why not work on, or at least diligently pray about, these issues now rather than let the miles rub them raw? Caring about your unborn baby means caring about the relationships that will matter most.

What specific steps could you take in the coming months to strengthen your key relationships? Take some time now to pray about any areas of unforgiveness or strain and ask for God's grace and wisdom.

_____

_____

_____

_____

_____

_____

_____

Do you have any special memories with your own grandparents? Tell your little one about them here.

_____

_____

_____

_____

_____

_____

True Beauty

*"The LORD does not look at the things
man looks at. Man looks at the outward
appearance, but the LORD looks at the heart."*

1 SAMUEL 16:7

Whether the scale has already skyrocketed or is just starting to inch up again after all the morning sickness, most pregnant women have some fears about the pounds they will pack on and how their bodies will change as a result of pregnancy. The good news is that all of the weight can come off quite naturally in the postpartum months. And while our bodies are made to shed all those pounds, on average, the permanent weight gain (the pounds that don't come off eventually after pregnancy) is between 2 and 4 pounds.

But whether your body changes for the heavier post-pregnancy or you find yourself dropping a size because of breast-feeding and keeping up with a toddler, here's something important to remember: people look at outward appearances, but God looks at your heart. And what does He see? Is it a heart growing in beauty as you become more giving and more forgiving? Or is it a heart that is growing harder and more callous?

It's not that we should let ourselves go when it comes to our physical appearance; after all, our bodies are God's temple. And outward beauty certainly reflects something of the order and loveliness of God in the world. But we should always remember that God places preeminent value on the state of our hearts. We should too.

What things does God find beautiful? Read 1 Peter 3:3–4. What do you think "a gentle and quiet spirit" looks like? How can we grow in these qualities?

_____

_____

_____

_____

_____

_____

_____

Dear Little One,

I have no idea right now what you will look like, but I do know about some of the qualities that God desires for your heart. I pray that you will be a person whose heart is known for . . .

_____

_____

_____

_____

_____

_____

_____

Hardening

Encourage one another daily, as long as
it is called Today, so that none of you
may be hardened by sin's deceitfulness.

HEBREWS 3:13

*I*nside your womb something amazing is happening. Cartilage is changing into bone. This process, known as ossification or bone material formation, begins now and continues in your body until the early twenties. (Make sure you are getting lots of calcium, by the way, because your little one will take what he or she needs from Mommy's bones if calcium demands aren't being met.)

When we talk about hardening in utero, it's usually a good thing. But there's lots of calcification, or hardening, that happens with adults that is not healthy. From kidney stones to arteriosclerosis (the hardening of the arteries), calcification in adults can be painful or deadly.

Spiritual hardening of the heart is described frequently throughout the Old and New Testaments. Pharaoh hardened his heart to the Lord's demands (Exodus 8:15). The Israelites hardened their hearts in the wilderness and later in exile (Psalm 95:7–9, Ezekiel 3:7). The book of Proverbs warns us, "Blessed is the man who always fears the LORD, but he who hardens his heart falls into trouble" (28:14). And Hebrews reminds believers to encourage one another, lest their hearts become "hardened by sin's deceitfulness" (3:13). Sin, you see, hardens the heart. And the more we sin, the more our sin leads to more sin, and the harder our hearts become. A repentant heart is a soft heart; it is pliable in the hands of God.

Is repentance a part of your daily time with God? It should be. Read through Psalm 53, one of the most famous passages of repentance in the Bible. What attitudes here should be emulated as we practice repentance in our own lives?

_____

_____

_____

_____

_____

_____

_____

Write a prayer for your baby's bone development. As you pray for his or her bones to grow hard, ask God to keep his or her spiritual heart soft and pliable to the things of God.

_____

_____

_____

_____

_____

_____

_____

Under Christ's Headship

God placed all things under his
feet and appointed him to be head
over everything for the church.

EPHESIANS 1:22

*A*s your baby's body grows, the central nervous system grows and gradually gains more control over all aspects of your baby's functioning. The central nervous system, or CNS (basically the head and spinal cord), will ultimately integrate the information it receives and coordinate and control the activity of all the body. Already your baby's CNS regulates the heartbeat and will soon manage your baby's response to stimuli.

Obviously, there's a good reason God chose the analogy of the head's control of the body to help us understand Christ's relationship with the church. The head controls, regulates, and makes possible all aspects of the body's functioning. Without the head, the body could not function. No matter how important one part of the body may seem, it is still under the head's control. No matter how insignificant one part of the body may seem, it is still vitally connected to the head. And without such connection, the body cannot work in an integrated, coordinated manner. Christ, the head, has supremacy over the body.

When we acknowledge Christ's supremacy over us, we recognize His right to direct our every thought and action. We do not begrudge Him lordship but instead recognize that we could not function independently from Him. For indeed, "in him we live and move and have our being" (Acts 17:28).

Write a prayer acknowledging and rejoicing in God's rightful authority over every aspect of your life. If there are parts of your life in which you have trouble submitting to His headship, acknowledge them and ask for His help in letting Him reign over all of you.

_____

_____

_____

_____

_____

_____

_____

Write out a prayer for the proper development of your baby's central nervous system. As you pray for brain and neural development, pray also that your baby will one day acknowledge Christ as head over every aspect of life.

_____

_____

_____

_____

_____

_____

WEEK 18

The Wonder Within

*I*n the next few weeks, you'll likely get a sneak peek of your little one—now about the size of a sweet potato (5.6 in. and 6.7 oz.). Your sweet "tater" may show off for the camera, demonstrating the new skills that he or she has been practicing: thumb sucking, grasping, yawning, or somersaulting. And while the doctors will be concerned with checking all aspects of baby's growing anatomy, you may be preoccupied with finding out the gender—that is, *if* you want to know. By this point, the technician should be able to tell you if you are having a boy or a girl—if your little one cooperates. Doing jumping jacks, drinking fruit juice, or even eating a candy bar might coax a stubborn one from a curled up position if necessary!

While your baby is barrel-rolling and pirouetting, you may be feeling like an old lady, with backaches and pains galore. Don't worry; you're not getting old. The hormone relaxin is loosening your joints and making room for Baby. Plus, the growing weight of your uterus, now the size of a melon, is pulling your back in and pushing your abdomen out—adding to your growing discomfort. If you're already feeling this, try soaking in a warm tub (just make sure the bath temperature isn't too hot). The tub will not only relieve some of those pains but also be a great place to practice relaxing for labor.

Points for Prayer and Praise

- Praise God for the opportunity we get in this era to see inside the womb through ultrasound. What an amazing gift it is to get a glimpse of life unfolding!
- Pray for your little one as he or she develops the grasping reflex. Pray also that one day your baby will grasp how much God loves him or her.
- Pray for inner peace and faith as you get ready to attend the upcoming anatomy scan. Pray that you and your spouse will completely trust in God and be able to glorify Him whether the scan reveals a normal, healthy baby or a potential problem.

Mommy's Memory Verse

Let us pursue the things which make for peace and the things by which one may edify another.

ROMANS 14:19 NKJV

Grasping for God

I pray that you, being rooted and established in love, may have power, together with all the saints, to grasp how wide and long and high and deep is the love of Christ, and to know this love that surpasses knowledge—that you may be filled to the measure of all the fullness of God.

EPHESIANS 3:17–19

*P*ractice, practice, practice: your little one is doing a lot of that this week. And one thing high on the practice list is grasping. You may even get a peek at this during the ultrasound: grabbing fingers, toes, even the umbilical cord. In a little more than twenty weeks, your baby will take that grasping reflex prime time, clutching your fingers, a rattle, big brother, or whatever comes within reach. And if you tickle the soles of those baby feet, even the toes will curl in a similar reflex.

This grasping reflex is a spiritual truth woven into creation. Saint Augustine may have put it best in *The Confessions* when he wrote, "You have made us for yourself, and our heart is restless until it rests in you."[2] All of us are born yearning for God even though we grasp after the wrong things and suppress our deepest yearning (Romans 1:18). But still our yearning is there. God wants us to grasp on to Him with everything we have. He wants us "to grasp how wide and long and high and deep" the love of Christ is. When we do, our emptiness will then, and only then, finally be filled.

Have you felt the restlessness Saint Augustine described? Have you tried to fill the void with other things besides God? Why is it that only God can satisfy our deepest longings?

_____

_____

_____

_____

_____

_____

_____

Until such time as your little one grasps on to God, you have the great responsibility of holding those tiny hands and lovingly leading your child toward Him. If the goal is to transfer those clasping hands from your own to the hand of God Himself, what habits and practices will you establish in your household to help toward that end?

_____

_____

_____

_____

_____

_____

_____

Whatever Comes

His disciples asked him, "Rabbi, who sinned,
this man or his parents, that he was born
blind?" "Neither this man nor his parents
sinned," said Jesus, "but this happened so that
the work of God might be displayed in his life."

JOHN 9:2–3

As the day drew near for our baby's twenty-week ultrasound, I was both giddy and fearful. I couldn't wait for the sneak peek at our little one, but I also couldn't help worrying that the ultrasound would reveal a genetic abnormality or problem. Try as I might, I couldn't block out this fear.

What if the ultrasound had revealed a serious medical issue? Though it would have taken some time to adjust to this new reality, the truth is that God would still have been at work glorifying Himself through the situation. As in the story of the blind beggar whom Jesus healed, I could have rested in the fact that "this happened so that the work of God might be displayed." I could also have rested in the truth that God would give me enough grace for each day He had given me with this little one.

Is your God big enough to carry you through whatever comes your way? Will you praise Him in the hard times as well as in the times of rejoicing? These words aren't meant to cause undue worry, but to spur us to cling to the truth of God's goodness no matter what trials come. They also remind us that every child is a gift.

Romans 8:28 says that God works all things—yes, all *things—together for the good of those who love Him and are called according to His purpose. How does this verse and today's opening verse give you courage to deal with whatever God brings you?*

_____

_____

_____

_____

_____

_____

Write a prayer for your baby's health, but also pray that God will give you grace should your little one be born with any sort of genetic abnormality or compromising medical condition. Pray that the works of God might be displayed in your life and the life of your child, no matter what.

_____

_____

_____

_____

_____

_____

Date:

- - - - - - - - - -

Left Out?

Let us pursue the things which make for peace
and the things by which one may edify another.

ROMANS 14:19 NKJV

Feeling your baby move for the first time is an experience like no other. It's hard to put words to just how amazing it is to feel the flutters of a tiny life inside you. All men are different, but for some husbands this can be a time when they feel a bit left out. It's understandable. They had their part to do in the baby making, got to be by your side when you squinted at a plus sign, and perhaps even held your hair back while you tossed your morning cookies. But now as Baby makes his or her presence felt, you alone get the thrill. And yes, if you're thinking that you deserve that perk after the morning sickness you suffered . . . you're right. But that's not the point. Love wants the good of the other no matter what.

"Let us make every effort to do what leads to peace and to mutual edification," the apostle Paul wrote. While your husband can't (and won't want to) experience every aspect of your pregnancy, make every effort to do what leads to peace in your household. For him, peace may mean getting the play-by-play of what you're experiencing, or it might mean you knowing when to just quit talking about it. Do what creates harmony in your house and encourages his spirit. Inasmuch as it depends on you, bless him today.

In what other ways can you help make sure your husband feels included in this expectant time?

_____

_____

_____

_____

_____

_____

In the book of Philippians, Paul prayed for the people's love to "abound more and more in knowledge and depth of insight" (1:9). The better we know someone, the better we can love someone. Write a prayer for your knowledge and insight into your child's personality and heart to grow deeper each year, so that you may in turn love him or her better with the passing of time.

_____

_____

_____

_____

_____

_____

Marriage Matters

*Come, my lover, let us go to the countryside,
let us spend the night in the villages. Let
us go early to the vineyards to see if the
vines have budded, if their blossoms have
opened, and if the pomegranates are in
bloom—there I will give you my love.*

SONG OF SONGS 7:11–12

*L*et's be honest. It's hard to read the Song of Songs in church without blushing. This book details the intimacy, ecstasy, and yes, sometimes the frustration and familiarity that are all a part of the marital bed. And while for centuries theologians avoided the literal applications of this book, they are certainly manifold.

Pregnancy affects us women and our husbands differently when it comes to how we feel about sexual closeness. Men may struggle with fears of hurting the baby or feel intense attraction to their wives. Women may feel unlovable or in full bloom. Wherever you find yourselves on this continuum, prioritize intimacy during these nine months. One of the best gifts you can give your children is a strong marriage. And intimacy—physical, emotional, and spiritual—is an enormous part of that. Now that morning sickness is (hopefully) over and before you get too close to your due date to travel, consider taking a lesson from Song of Songs. Here's a memory verse you probably never had to learn, but might be good to say to your sweetie: "Come, my lover, let us go to the countryside . . ."

God created man and woman for intimate relationship. Likewise, he created us both to need an intimate connection with Himself. In what ways could you work on pursuing a deeper intimacy with God?

_____

_____

_____

_____

_____

_____

_____

_____

If you could plan a getaway with your husband before the baby comes, where would you go?

_____

_____

_____

_____

_____

_____

_____

WEEK 19

The Wonder Within

As we continue moving on up the produce aisle of pregnancy, your little one weighs in this week at around 8.5 ounces and stretches out to around 6 inches long, roughly the size of a mango. Your sweet little mango now has arms and legs in proportion—and you are likely feeling those perfectly proportioned karate chops and kicks! Meanwhile, a white, cheeselike substance known as the vernix caseosa is beginning to cover baby's skin. In His infinite wisdom God designed this white, pasty coating to protect the fetus while immersed in amniotic fluid. In most cases the vernix caseosa disappears almost completely by birth.

Speaking of skin, yours may be feeling a bit itchy these days now that it is beginning to stretch. That's normal. Use a non-alcohol-based cream or body butter (since alcohol dries the skin) with coconut oil and/or shea butter. Some research has shown that creams infused with vitamin E may play some small role in preventing stretch marks. A steady rate of weight gain can also help to minimize their appearance. If you do get them, wear them as a badge of honor. God made your body to house this kind of miracle, and if our bodies are stretched and worn in the process, we wear the stripes as a testimony of both our sacrifice and love.

POINTS FOR PRAYER AND PRAISE

🍼 Praise God for the way He protects your little one—from the vernix caseosa, which covers the skin, to the cushion of the amniotic fluid, to the protective design of the uterus. God has prepared a safe place for your baby. Praise Him that His hand of protection is also on you.

🍼 Pray for your little one's developing senses. Pray that one day he or she might have a vision for Christ and a taste for the things of God.

🍼 Pray for wisdom as you and your spouse choose a name for your baby. And pray that God would be honored in your decision.

MOMMY'S MEMORY VERSE

Pray continually.

1 THESSALONIANS 5:17

Hungry Souls

Pray continually.

1 THESSALONIANS 5:17

As I write this particular entry, I'm thirty-two weeks pregnant. Already this morning, I had a bagel around 8, an apple at 10, a sandwich at 11:30, and a granola bar at 12:30. I'm trying to figure out what to eat next (the fridge is bare) because I'm still so hungry. And I'll be honest, even though it's the middle of the day, the mint chocolate chip ice cream is beckoning.

Sometimes when you're pregnant you feel like you could eat around the clock. And honestly, it's not such a bad idea. Small frequent meals are better for your digestive system, which—as you've probably begun to discover—is working super slowly, causing the unfortunate side effect of frequent heartburn. Plus, as baby gets bigger, your stomach gets smaller.

Round-the-clock mini-meals aren't such a bad idea when it comes to your spiritual life either. It's not enough to get fueled up with a quiet time in the morning and go on spiritual autopilot for the rest of the day. In the Old Testament we see men like Daniel taking regular times out to pray. In the New Testament Paul commanded us to pray without ceasing. And throughout church history we see different ways Christians have tried to make spiritual practices more than once-a-day add-ons. Whether it's praying at mealtimes or praying the hours like the Benedictine monks, Christians have recognized a need to be continually in God's presence. How about you?

Is there anything that would help you make talking to God a more frequent part of your day? Posting Scripture verses, making mealtime grace more than just a formality, making prayer walks a regular habit—what practices could you incorporate to learn to pray and keep fellowship with God continually? Brainstorm here.

_____

_____

_____

_____

_____

_____

Once your little one arrives, he or she will be eating around the clock too. Whether you are breast-feeding, bottle-feeding, or a combination of both, those feeding times create built-in space to stop. Make a habit of using some of that downtime to pray or even meditate on Scripture. Brainstorm how you could help yourself inculcate this habit (such as writing Scripture verses on index cards or downloading the Bible for one-handed reading on an e-reader). Get creative!

_____

_____

_____

_____

_____

Picture Book

*This is a profound mystery—but I am
talking about Christ and the church.*

EPHESIANS 5:32

Goodnight Moon, The Very Hungry Caterpillar, Pat the Bunny—you may already be beginning your collection of picture books for your little one. These first board books are simple stories driven more by pictures than by words. And yet, some of them we remember fondly for life.

God has already picked out your child's very first picture book. In Ephesians Paul told us that marriage is a picture of Christ and His church. Each day of your child's life, he or she will be closely examining the pictures in this unfolding story. If your marriage reflects what Paul described, your little one will see a picture of Christ who is both leader and servant, loving His bride so much that He lays down His life for her on a daily basis. Your little one will also see a picture of the church as respecting Christ, submitting to and serving Him out of love, and living selflessly for His sake. No marriage reflects this perfectly, but every marriage is painting a picture for good or for ill of what Christ and His church look like.

One of the best things you can do now for your little one's future spiritual life is to work on your marriage. And the truth is, while you can pray for your husband, you can only be responsible for how well you are reflecting your part of what Paul called this "profound mystery."

Read over Ephesians 5:21–33. What are the key attitudes and actions describing husbands and wives? Pray for your marriage to exhibit these qualities. Ask God to convict you of any sin in your relationship with your husband and to help you think of any specific ways you can improve your attitude or actions toward him.

_____

_____

_____

_____

_____

_____

_____

Have you started collecting any books for your little one? Do you have any special childhood books that were your favorites? Tell about them here.

_____

_____

_____

_____

_____

_____

_____

What's in a Name?

A good name is better than fine perfume.

ECCLESIASTES 7:1

*I*n biblical times names carried great significance. Names could represent a person's destiny or character. For this reason, God gave special attention to people's names, going so far as to change the names of such important figures as Abram (Abraham), Sarai (Sarah), Jacob (Israel), Simon (Peter), and Saul (Paul). To name someone or something was to exercise authority over that person or creation, so God's renaming of people was also a sign of His authority over their lives. And to be sent or to speak in someone's name meant to go with His authority (Jeremiah 11:21, 2 Corinthians 5:20). When we go in Jesus' name, we go with His authority. And to forget God's name was to depart from Him (Jeremiah 23:27).

Because God gives such credence to names, it bears considering that we also should choose names mindfully. God's Word certainly doesn't offer a how-to guide on naming, and in the Bible's silence, we shouldn't add more than what is said. But the importance of names in the Bible does give us a precedent to consider: names carry more significance than the sum of a few sounds. As you work on a name list for your child, do so in an attitude of prayer. Ask God to lead you to choose a name for your little one that will honor Him.

When Jesus gave the Great Commission, He told the disciples to baptize people in the name of the Father, the Son, and the Holy

Spirit. Being baptized in the name of Jesus testifies to the world that we submit to God's authority and that we identify ourselves as His followers. What confidence do you draw from the fact that you are under God's authority and are so closely connected with Him that you share in His name?

_____

_____

_____

_____

_____

_____

_____

Have you started considering any names yet? If so, which ones are on the list so far?

_____

_____

_____

_____

_____

_____

_____

Date:

Preparing a Place

"In My Father's house are many mansions;
if it were not so, I would have told you.
I go to prepare a place for you."

JOHN 14:2 NKJV

*M*isty Sea Foam, Iced Mocha, Tickled Pink, Summer Blue—maybe you've already started collecting those paint samples, holding them up to the wall, and daydreaming about a space for your little one. Planning a nursery for your bundle of joy is one of those activities that can happily keep you up late at night. Will it be ladybugs or fire trucks that cruise across those baby sheets? Whatever your personal style, you have a blank canvas to splash your creativity onto, and half the fun is dreaming about bringing your little one home to your lovingly prepared nest. (Of course, if a new nursery just isn't within the scope of your budget or size of your house, don't sweat it. Your baby won't know the difference!)

As I think about how much joy I've gotten from decorating a room for my little ones, my mind quickly goes to how much joy Christ must take in preparing a heavenly place for us. What delight He must have in knowing that one day soon He will bring us to a place where there is no more pain, tears, sin, or death! He knows us through and through and is preparing a place with us specifically in mind. This will be a place that provides for every longing for true rest we've ever had; the unsettledness here on earth we could never quite shake off; and our insatiable ache for belonging. What joy He will have when He brings us home!

How does it make you feel to think about Christ preparing such a grand place for you?

_____

_____

_____

_____

_____

_____

_____

Have you already been thinking about the nursery? Tell your little one about some of your thoughts or projects you've started. Or maybe it's still a ways off for you. If that's the case, come back to this entry later.

_____

_____

_____

_____

_____

_____

_____

WEEK 20

The Wonder Within

*T*hough your little one is about one-eighth of the size he or she will be at birth, all major organs are developed by now. At the anatomy scan, the doctor will be checking to see that vital organs, such as the heart, the kidneys, and the primitive lungs, are functioning as they should be at this stage in development. Though there is still much growing left to do, your little one already stretches out to around 10 inches—about the size of a banana—from crown to heel and weighs 10.6 ounces. (Note that around the twenty-week mark, babies are measured from head to heel rather than crown to rump.)

As for you, by God's grace, you've reached the halfway point of pregnancy. Congratulations on making it through the trials of morning sickness, nausea, and aversions. By now, the top of your uterus is right about parallel to your belly button. And you are getting to know and recognize the rhythms of your little kickboxer. You aren't alone if you notice him or her moving mostly at night (of course *after* you've finally laid down to rest!) or that the motion of your movement during the daytime—the sway of your hips when you walk—gently lulls Baby to sleep. That's a good thing to remember once your baby arrives in about twenty weeks, especially if you find him or her difficult to soothe. That's why mothers of newborns so often find a gentle swaying motion will soothe a fussy baby; it reminds Baby of life in utero.

Points for Prayer and Praise

- Praise God for seeing you and Baby through the first half of your pregnancy.
- Pray for the results of the anatomy scan to come back showing a healthy baby if this is the Lord's will for you and your family.
- Pray for God to strengthen your marriage as you prepare for your baby's arrival. Pray in particular that God will help you both be selfless, forgiving, and encouraging toward each other in the pursuit of virtue.

Mommy's Memory Verse

My frame was not hidden from you when I was made in the secret place. When I was woven together in the depths of the earth, your eyes saw my unformed body.

PSALM 139:15–16

God's Claim

*My frame was not hidden from you when
I was made in the secret place. When I
was woven together in the depths of the
earth, your eyes saw my unformed body.*

PSALM 139:15–16

*W*e could have watched all day. As the technician moved the wand over my belly, the screen showed the curve of our son. He was curled up, relaxing atop the cushion of Mommy's bladder. We marveled at the staircase of his spine, the contours of his profile, and the little hands that moved up to his lips. *Was he sucking his thumb?* we wondered.

Leaving the clinic and clutching a handful of snapshot souvenirs, I couldn't help but feel sad that I would have to wait twenty weeks for another glimpse of my son. While the average mother may get one or two short windows into the womb through ultrasound, God's view is direct and uninterrupted. That which is veiled to our eyes is constantly before His. He orchestrates and sees every development. He smiles at the sight of somersaults, barrel rolls, and karate kicks that we only feel.

As your child grows through life, you will always feel a special bond. After all, you carried that life within you for nine (plus) months. That child is your own flesh and blood. But this passage reminds us that God not only knows your child long before you do, but that He created your child. He knows every nerve and sinew of your child's body. As Creator, Father, and Sustainer, He has a love and a claim over your child greater than your own. This child will be cradled in your arms soon, but for now he or she knows the intimacy of just one constant gaze of love: that of our heavenly Father.

Jeremiah 1:5 says, "Before I formed you in the womb I knew you." How does it make you feel to realize the intimate view and knowledge God has of your growing baby?

_____

_____

_____

_____

_____

_____

Write a prayer for your baby. Ask God to graciously let this first relationship—the one with Him—be the defining relationship of your son's or daughter's life.

_____

_____

_____

_____

_____

_____

_____

Boy or Girl?

God created man in his own image,
in the image of God he created him;
male and female he created them.

GENESIS 1:27

*E*veryone's been asking you lately, "So, do you know whether you're having a boy or a girl?" Whether the news comes now or at birth, it's very common to have some degree of gender disappointment or perhaps anxiety. You may feel more prepared to care for a boy or a girl. Or the quiet dreams you've been dreaming since childhood may revolve around ballet recitals for your sweet baby girl or camping trips with your rambunctious boy cub.

Whether you bring home a bundle of pink or blue, you can trust that God particularly chose you as the mother of this girl or boy. And your baby's gender is no surprise to Him. He knows the baby He has blessed you with particularly needs you as his or her mother. He also knows the world will need this someday man or woman.

The Bible also teaches us that both sexes are made in the image of God. Some of the ways in which men and women reflect the image of God are the same, and some are different, but taken together, they give us a fuller picture of the God whom we worship and enjoy. Your child will be a special glimpse of the glory of God, so you can be sure He is giving you and the world in which you live that unique glimpse of His glory for a purpose.

Write down some glimpses of God's glory you have seen in the children you know. List examples from both genders.

_____

_____

_____

_____

_____

_____

_____

Share with your child about your decision to find out his or her gender at the ultrasound or to wait until birth. What led you to that decision? Did you and Dad feel differently about it? Did either of you have to convince the other?

_____

_____

_____

_____

_____

_____

_____

Motive Check

If I speak in the tongues of men and of angels,
but have not love, I am only a resounding gong or
a clanging cymbal. If I have the gift of prophecy
and can fathom all mysteries and all knowledge,
and if I have a faith that can move mountains,
but have not love, I am nothing. If I give all I
possess to the poor and surrender my body to
the flames, but have not love, I gain nothing.

1 CORINTHIANS 13:1–3

One of the best things you can do for your baby before he or she comes is to spend some time strengthening your marriage. As you work on truly loving your spouse the way God intends, you will also learn many important lessons about loving your children.

In his introduction to the Love Chapter, Paul emphasized with the grandest brushstrokes that our efforts, no matter how splashy they may be, are useless if applied without the right motive: love. We may move mountains and give all that we have, but if we do it with the wrong motive, it is meaningless.

What is your motive for loving your husband? Do you love him so that you will be loved in return? All of us want our love reciprocated, but the key to loving well is to do so not for your own sake, but rather as an act of worship to God. When you love because of your love for God, there is no condition standing between you and your spouse, and your well will not run dry.

When we love to be loved in return, we often grow resentful if our expressions are not equally reciprocated or even noticed. We will often hold a measuring stick to our spouse's behavior. How does loving your spouse as an act of worship to God change this?

_____

_____

_____

_____

_____

_____

How does this same lesson apply to loving our children? How does loving them as an act of worship free us up to love them well and love them without resentment?

_____

_____

_____

_____

_____

_____

_____

Patient Partners, Patient Parents

*Love is patient, love is kind. It does not
envy, it does not boast, it is not proud.*

1 CORINTHIANS 13:4

If there is one quality you will need in abundance as you raise the little one you are carrying, it is the gift of patience. (While it may seem light-years in the distance, before you know it you will wonder how many times you must discipline the same behavior, repeat your instructions, or hear your little one whine over something withheld.) And as we continue to look at how to make our marriages strong enough to thrive during the child-rearing years, patience is high on that list too.

If there is anyone with whom we ought to be able to be patient, it ought to be our husbands. While we can't choose our parents or our children we're given, we do choose our spouses. And yet, even with our husbands, we can't help but be impatient.

In every marriage there are areas where patience just runs thin. You've probably had many conversations about those areas, whether they are small (like caked-on cereal dishes in the sink) or large (like making huge expenditures without talking about them together first). Whether it's merely a pet peeve or an outright issue of sin, we still must learn to cultivate patience both with our husbands and with God's timeline for when or if change is to happen.

In whatever situations we lose patience, we will always be more successful praying about those areas rather than nagging our husbands about them. We can't change others; only God can. And as we present our requests and concerns to God in prayer, He will first convict us of our own ways that need changing before He leads us to remove the specks from the eyes of our husbands.

Think of one way—just this week—you disappointed God. How did He show patience toward you? Take time now to ask His help with extending patience toward your spouse and children.

_____

_____

_____

_____

_____

Patience is really about waiting on God's timing to bring change and trusting Him in the time of waiting. Think about a time when you've had to be patient. What kind of character-building work did God do in you or in others through that time of waiting?

_____

_____

_____

_____

_____

WEEK 21

The Wonder Within

*T*his week your little wonder is about the length of a carrot (10.5 in.) and weighs approximately 12.7 ounces, making him or her about as thin as a carrot stick too. He or she will begin to accumulate brown fat—a kind of fat that helps regulate the body temperature both now and in the critical first few weeks of life. Your baby will also soon begin developing rapid eye movement, or REM. While this is an important step in sleep development, it also means that baby is now capable of dreaming. Amazing, huh?

Speaking of dreaming, you may be finding yourself dreaming in Technicolor these days. Pregnant women report some very unusual and vivid dreams. While pregnant women have less REM sleep (the kind in which dreaming occurs) than other women, they are also waking more frequently (between midnight potty runs, those excruciating leg cramps, and trying to find a comfortable sleeping position). Hormonal surges, particularly that of progesterone, can also result in more memorable dreams, while the heightened emotions of pregnancy may give plenty of fodder for anxious dreams. If your dreams are running wild, even scaring you, don't hesitate to pray over them. God is Lord of both day and night, and certainly capable of guarding your dreams.

Points for Prayer and Praise

🍼 Praise God for the gender of your child (whether you know what it is or not). Praise Him that He makes no mistakes and thank Him that He has chosen you, in particular, to raise this boy or girl.

🍼 Pray for your little one as he or she develops REM sleep and the ability to dream. Pray also that one day his or her life dreams and ambitions would be glorifying to God.

🍼 Pray for God to strengthen your marriage in the months before the baby comes—particularly that you and your husband might exhibit patience, kindness, and humility toward each other and that envy and boasting will have no place in your home.

Mommy's Memory Verse

Love is patient, love is kind. It does not envy, it does not boast, it is not proud.

1 Corinthians 13:4

Kindness in the Crucible

*Love is patient, love is kind. It does not
envy, it does not boast, it is not proud.*

1 CORINTHIANS 13:4

Although simple, the second greatest commandment—love your neighbor as yourself—is far from easy.

When you chose the man you would marry, it is as if God gave you one person to practice fleshing out this great command. If within the crucible of marriage you could learn to love someone you chose, you will inevitably learn to care (with a different type of love, of course) for those whom you did not choose—your children, your neighbors, even your enemies. As you practice this simple but strenuous command with your spouse, you are also building skills for loving your children well.

Twenty-four hours a day, seven days a week, you are called to one task: love your husband as yourself. And kindness is certainly at the heart of that love. Kindness may not sound hard, but sometimes in our familiarity we grow lax in the most basic labors of love: courtesy, gentleness, compassion, deference, and empathy. We expect much without first being liberal in our own selflessness. And as a result, resentment creeps in and nests in our hearts—and in our husband's.

In the Old Testament, kindness was synonymous with God's faithfulness to His covenants made with His people. In our marriages, kindness is at the heart of covenant faithfulness. To practice kindness in our words, in our tone, in our actions, and in our thoughts toward our husbands is to preserve the covenant we made with him.

How can you show your husband kindness today? Is there an area in which he especially needs understanding and empathy from you? How could you imitate the bounty and lavishness of God in your kindness to him?

_____

_____

_____

_____

_____

_____

_____

Write a prayer for your son or daughter to develop a kind heart. In your prayer, ask God for His grace to help you model for your children His kindness.

_____

_____

_____

_____

_____

_____

_____

Date:

- - - - - - - - - - -

Forgetting the Joneses

Love is patient, love is kind. It does not
envy, it does not boast, it is not proud.

1 CORINTHIANS 13:4

*I*t's so subtle we may hardly even realize it, but many a marriage problem begins with the Joneses—trying to keep up with them or trying to impress them. The Jones's new car and fine house make you ungrateful for the car and house you already have. Suddenly, your previously wonderful husband is not working hard enough, isn't smart enough, or just doesn't have enough ambition. Or consider the last time you slapped down your credit card and ran up a bill you couldn't afford. Was it for something you really needed, or was it for something you wanted so you could impress or keep up with others? Before you know it, your spending is dividing you and your spouse. How much heartache could be saved if you'd just forget the Joneses!

Gratitude is the antidote to envy. So make gratitude, especially for the little things, a daily practice. Reflect on the true source of any blessing you have. Likewise, realizing your absolute dependence on God is the antidote to boasting. So acknowledge your dependence on Him in all that you do. As we tame both beasts of envy and boasting, we come to learn the secret of contentment. Contentment will go a long way toward creating a happy marriage. And it will prepare you well for raising children who are a pleasure to be around—neither sulking because they don't have the latest toy, nor peacocking about their talents or possessions. Love your spouse and your future children by jettisoning the Joneses.

In what areas do you find yourself preoccupied with appearances? How can those areas negatively affect your marriage and home? Pray that God would give you a heart that is more set on pleasing Him than impressing others.

_____

_____

_____

_____

_____

_____

Write a prayer for God's help in teaching (and modeling) contentment to your child. Pray that the Lord would help you as you train in areas such as sharing, waiting for a turn, and not whining. Pray that you would be an example of contentment.

_____

_____

_____

_____

_____

_____

_____

The Pride Problem

*Love is patient, love is kind. It does not
envy, it does not boast, it is not proud.*

1 CORINTHIANS 13:4

*W*hen it comes to marriage, pride is a wrecking ball. Pride makes us see our needs and wants as more important than another's. Pride makes us sure we are in the right and the other is in the wrong. Pride blinds us: it makes it hard to see another's struggles, joys, needs, or strengths. A proud person is rarely a servant unless she's serving in a way that trumpets her own sacrifice and inflates her own ego. Worst of all, the prouder we are, the harder it is to be yielded to God or to another.

But where humility graces a marriage, so too enters understanding, compassion, forgiveness, sensitivity, service, and submission. A humble person is so filled with God, so caught up in the grandeur of God and in the satisfaction of knowing Him, that she can be emptied of preoccupation with herself. A humble person listens instead of concluding her way is best. A humble person yields to the preference of another rather than trampling his desires. A humble person hopes for the best from another rather than expecting the worst.

We will never rid ourselves completely of pride on this side of heaven. But the more we expel pride from our hearts, the better we equip ourselves to truly love—not just our husbands, but our children and neighbors as well. As we humble ourselves before God, He does the surgery our hearts most desperately need: emptying us of self so we may be full of Him.

Pride blinds us to our own shortcomings. Write a prayer asking God to open your eyes to areas where your pride is getting in the way of a healthy relationship with your husband.

_____

_____

_____

_____

_____

_____

_____

_____

How can pride cripple your ability to parent well? Why is humility a good trait for parents to possess?

_____

_____

_____

_____

_____

_____

_____

_____

After You

[Love] is not rude, it is not self-
seeking, it is not easily angered,
it keeps no record of wrongs.

1 CORINTHIANS 13:5

Children forever alter marriages. In God's design, this alteration is a good thing, not a bad one. Inasmuch as marriage itself begins to teach us about putting another's needs before our own, the arrival of children takes that lesson to a higher level. Love, Paul told us, is by its very nature "not self-seeking." And what better way is there to begin learning the heart of love than to enter into an experience that calls—in fact, compels—us to put another's needs before our own?

But putting others' needs before our own is easier said than done. And certainly the selflessness that is involved in raising children stretches many parents and marriages to their breaking points. That's why as you prepare your marriage for the arrival of this child, whether this is your first or your fourth, pray that God would help you and your spouse be as Christ in His selflessness, in His servant's heart.

A servant's heart can begin developing now as you put the needs of your spouse above your own. Can you put your own agenda aside long enough to listen to and join in on what's important to your husband? And can you take the time you had planned to spend on yourself and instead lavish that time praying for your husband, that you would both grow in the selflessness that parenting demands?

In what ways does your husband demonstrate selfless love to you? How do you demonstrate selfless love to him?

_____

_____

_____

_____

_____

_____

_____

Write a prayer for yourself and your husband that you will grow in this aspect of love.

_____

_____

_____

_____

_____

_____

_____

WEEK 22

The Wonder Within

*D*oes it feel like your little gymnast is practicing for the Olympics these days? If you feel like there are somersaults, cartwheels, and flips going on inside you, it's probably because Baby is exploring the space around him or her. And your little explorer—now about as long as a cucumber (10.9 in.) and weighing close to a pound—is aided by a developing sense of balance, compliments of the final development of the inner ear. Your little one is experiencing a world of sensation as he or she moves through the amniotic fluid, grasps the umbilical cord, and steps against the walls of your uterus. Nerve cells to the brain are registering a world of exciting sensory experiences.

While your gymnast is cavorting around the uterine jungle gym, you may be the one feeling out of breath. Many women report feeling shortness of breath beginning in this stage of pregnancy. If you've begun to experience this, know that you are not breathing more frequently, you're just inhaling and exhaling more in terms of volume. As your pregnancy progresses, you'll notice this shortness of breath increasing as the top of your uterus pushes up against your lungs. But for now, the top of your uterus is still a good distance away—about 2 inches above your navel. That's enough growth, however, to give you a cute little baby bump. Enjoy it!

Points for Prayer and Praise

- Praise God for giving you the opportunity to be a mother. What an enormous privilege and responsibility. Thank Him for these precious days and the ones to come.
- Pray for your little one as he or she develops a sense of balance. Pray also that as your little one grows, his or her priorities in life will reflect the balance that God intends.
- Pray for God to be *the* source of strength in your marriage before Baby comes—particularly that you and your spouse would be slow to anger and quick to forgive.

Mommy's Memory Verse

[Love] is not rude, it is not self-seeking, it is not easily angered, it keeps no record of wrongs. Love does not delight in evil but rejoices with the truth.

1 Corinthians 13:5–6

Unflappable

[Love] is not rude, it is not self-seeking, it is not easily angered, it keeps no record of wrongs.

1 CORINTHIANS 13:5

*H*ealthy parenting starts with healthy marriages. As we continue to look at ways in which we can baby-proof our marriages, we turn our attention to anger. How do you react when your husband says something that hurts you, forgets something important to you, or otherwise misses the mark? Do you sting him with words? Do you become icy while maintaining that "nothing's wrong"? Do you bottle it up and then explode in a litany of wrongs?

Love isn't easily irritated. It assumes the best. It considers it possible that we have misjudged the other's motives. Love seeks reconciliation (Matthew 5:23–24). Love is calm, gentle, and patient.

Let's face it: every marriage needs these qualities in the face of children. If we have first practiced with our spouses, how much better will we keep our cool with the toddler who willfully flings the mashed potatoes, with the nine-year-old who calls home for the fifth day in a row to say he forgot his lunch, or with the teen whose words wound us to the core?

But how do we develop this spirit? In part, it's learning that our value comes not from our spouses or children, but from God. When we are secure in God's love, we will be unflappable when others let us down. When we are secure in the love of God, we can give mercy even when wronged.

*What is your response style when it comes to anger? Do you
bottle things up, or do you easily explode? Why are both extremes
unhealthy?*

_____

_____

_____

_____

_____

_____

_____

*Write a prayer confessing your need for God's help when
provoked. Ask for His help with being slow to anger and calm in
spirit.*

_____

_____

_____

_____

_____

_____

_____

Keeping Score

[Love] is not rude, it is not self-seeking, it is not easily angered, it keeps no record of wrongs.

1 CORINTHIANS 13:5

*I*f there is anything that will dismantle your marriage and divide two people who desperately need to be on the same team, it's resentment and unforgiveness. Love keeps no record of wrongs. When baby-proofing your marriage, start by looking at that list you've been keeping. You know the one: the time he forgot the date night you'd planned and worked late, the unkind remark that still chafes, or the Saturday he spent watching football when you'd asked for his help. Or maybe the list has much bigger things you just aren't willing to forgive. Either way, the list is toxic, and it will slowly corrode your relationship.

There is a better way. In matters that are too important to overlook, don't bury them; seek reconciliation, even godly counsel if necessary. And whether or not your spouse apologizes, work toward forgiveness. In the small things, work on letting them go (1 Peter 4:8). The bottom line is, you married a sinner. Furthermore, *you* are a sinner. You will let one another down in countless ways over the course of your marriage. The question is, will you give grace or will you demand perfection that you yourself cannot even meet?

Tackle this now before there's a new baby on the scene and you're tempted to keep score over who changed the last diaper or got up with baby most. Throw the scoreboard out before you bring home Baby.

Imagine if God kept a list of all your wrongs and brought it up whenever you stumbled. How do you think that might affect your relationship with Him?

_____

_____

_____

_____

_____

_____

When a mother sacrifices a lot and is making those sacrifices for the wrong reasons, it's easy for resentment toward her husband to build. For whom do we ultimately do our work? How does working unto the Lord keep resentment from being an issue?

_____

_____

_____

_____

_____

_____

_____

Of Vice and Virtue

*Love does not delight in evil but
rejoices with the truth.*

1 CORINTHIANS 13:6

Is there a sin in your life that you're secretly relieved your husband also indulges in? Maybe you're given to laziness. Do you quietly encourage the same tendencies in your husband? Maybe you gossip or have a critical tongue. Do you find a sick satisfaction when you both criticize someone behind his or her back? Or does it grieve you to see your husband falling prey to any sin? Do you long to see him grow in godliness and to lead you and your family in a way that constantly puts to death the sin in both your lives?

God wants our marriages to be places where iron sharpens iron. He wants us to be constantly cheering each other on toward higher plateaus of holiness. But that won't happen unless we truly grieve over sin in our own lives. The more we hate evil and hunger for righteousness, the better spiritual helpmates we can be.

Not only will this principle strengthen your marriage before Baby comes, it will also help you lead your children to grow in virtue and break the pattern of your vices. It's inevitable that you will sin before and against your own children. Will they see a mom who delights in snide comments? Will they see a mom who never says, "I'm sorry"? Or will they see a mom who is quick to grieve her own sin, ask forgiveness, and make amends?

Think about any areas where you may influence your spouse to sin. Have you ever truly grieved over that sin and confessed it to God and to your husband? Pray over those areas. Then write about an area where you could encourage virtue in your husband.

_____

_____

_____

_____

_____

_____

_____

Do you think it will be hard to say "I'm sorry" to your child? Write a prayer asking God to make you quick to repent and vulnerable enough to apologize and ask forgiveness when you fail him or her.

_____

_____

_____

_____

_____

_____

_____

Protector

[Love] always protects, always trusts,
always hopes, always perseveres.

1 CORINTHIANS 13:7

*W*hen it comes to the role of protector, we often think of it as the husband's job. And while husbands certainly do have that role, this passage in 1 Corinthians 13 lets us know that protecting is part of the job description for *all* who love.

So what might it look like for a wife to protect her husband? Emotionally, a wife protects her husband by not bad-mouthing him— not even to her girlfriends. She protects him emotionally by being there for him and listening. Physically, a wife protects her husband by being sexually available to him and by keeping her own body in a way that is alluring to him. Physically, she can also do a lot to protect his health: suggesting active family outings, cooking healthy meals if she's the one typically doing meal preparation, and encouraging him to take time for a pickup basketball game or a run. Spiritually, a wife who knows the Word of God and whose faith is strong, even when circumstances are bleak, protects her family. She is willing to confront her husband if he is leading the family into sin, and she buttresses his faith when times are hard.

These protective moves will go a long way toward creating a solid marriage—one that will be a safe haven for your children. A wife has an active role in protecting her marriage and family. Accept that challenge.

Brainstorm other ways in which God might be calling you to actively protect your marriage and family. Make a list here.

_____

_____

_____

_____

_____

_____

_____

_____

In what ways do you anticipate protecting your future son or daughter in physical, emotional, and spiritual realms?

_____

_____

_____

_____

_____

_____

_____

WEEK 23

The Wonder Within

A car alarm goes off and the neighborhood dogs begin barking furiously. You startle and, at the same time, your baby does as well. That's because your little one—now about the length of an eggplant (11.38 in.) and weighing a little over a pound—has a developed enough sense of hearing that he or she can sense sounds both inside and outside the womb. Regular sounds like the gurgling of your stomach, the lilt of your voice, and the whoosh of your blood flow are the soundtrack to your baby's days. Your little one can also sense light and dark at this point, though those pretty little eyes will not open (remember those fused eyelids?) for another week or two.

With your little one's hearing developing so rapidly, make sure you are taking time to talk, read, and even sing to your baby. Your voice will be a source of comfort and a constant in his or her life. And now's a great time to increase bonding by singing lullabies or chattering sweet words to the one tucked beneath your heart. It's also a great way for your husband to feel involved on your pregnancy journey. So grab a book—maybe your favorite children's book or even favorite book of the Bible—and read aloud to your little one. It's a habit you'll be reinforcing for life.

POINTS FOR PRAYER AND PRAISE

- Have you gotten back the results of your anatomy scan yet? If so, praise God for the healthy formation of your son or daughter. And if there are causes for concern, take those to Him in prayer, remembering that every child is a gift.

- Pray for your baby's developing sense of hearing. And also pray that your little one will learn to know the voice of God the Father and follow His voice always.

- Pray for God to continue strengthening your marriage before Baby comes. Pray in particular that you and your spouse will love each other with a protecting, trusting, hoping, and persevering kind of love—a love that will remain.

MOMMY'S MEMORY VERSE

[Love] always protects, always trusts, always hopes, always perseveres. Love never fails.

1 CORINTHIANS 13:7–8

Expect the Best

*[Love] always protects, always trusts,
always hopes, always perseveres.*

1 CORINTHIANS 13:7

*O*ftentimes after we've lived closely with someone (like a spouse), we begin to assume that we can predict their behavior, especially when it's in relation to something negative. We may even begin to talk to our husband in a way that reflects our predictions: "Never mind, I know you won't do it the way I want it done" or "I know you won't make it on time so I'll just go by myself."

But Paul told us that real love expects the best from the beloved. And even when we've been let down, real love trusts. Of course there are some cases when a wife should protect herself—in cases of physical abuse or when a husband is being unfaithful. But Paul's counsel was addressing a general posture of expecting the best from someone's character rather than the worst.

Let's say, for instance, that your husband said he would be on time for your doctor's appointment, but the nurse is now calling your name and he's nowhere in sight. Do you mutter in exasperation, "I knew he'd be late; he just doesn't care"? Or do you expect the best of him, thinking, *Perhaps he got caught in heavy traffic.* The heart that expects the worst will give him a tongue-lashing when he walks in the door. The heart that expects the best will listen and be gracious. When disappointed, real love has the ability to keep a soft heart and to look to the Lord in hope that He can bring about change.

Ask God to forgive you for the ways in which you've expected the worst of your husband. How do you think expecting the best of your husband fosters positive results?

_____

_____

_____

_____

_____

_____

_____

_____

How does a child feel differently about himself or herself depending upon whether a parent expects the best or the worst?

_____

_____

_____

_____

_____

_____

_____

_____

_____

How Strong Is Your God?

*[Love] always protects, always trusts,
always hopes, always perseveres.*

1 CORINTHIANS 13:7

*H*ave you given up hope in some aspect of your marriage? Have you resigned yourself to a conclusion that some things will just never get better? Or have you taken matters into your own hands and nagged constantly about something? Your response says a lot about your view of God and your view of man. Is God capable of bringing about change in your marriage? Absolutely! Are we as people capable of changing? Yes, by the grace—and only by the grace—of God.

When we've been hoping for something to change for a while and it hasn't, it's easy to grow cynical or just depressed. Proverbs 13:12 says, "Hope deferred makes the heart sick." Indeed, there's nothing quite as souring to the stomach as hoping, truly hoping, for a change and being disappointed.

But the good news is, we serve a mighty God. In His hands we are like clay. And like the thief who hung beside Jesus on the cross, change is possible even in our final hour. But change, especially in another person, doesn't come about through our own efforts, such as nagging or leaving self-help books lying around. We can't change someone else. It's a matter between the other person and God. We can pray, asking God to work that person's life toward change for the better, but we must always remember such change is truly a gift. And because our God is all-good and all-powerful, we do not give up hope, but petition Him in hope and in faith.

Think about an area where you desire to see change in your marriage. Have you prayed consistently about it? Write out this affirmation and sign and date it: "I refuse to give up hope for any aspect of my marriage. I am willing to commit this to God and actively pray for His gift of change."

_____

_____

_____

_____

_____

_____

_____

How could this same lesson be applied to raising the little one you are now carrying in your womb?

_____

_____

_____

_____

_____

_____

Persevering Love

[Love] always protects, always trusts,
always hopes, always perseveres.

1 CORINTHIANS 13:7

Perseverance isn't an easy thing. It's easy to love when we are loved well in return. But when love gets tough, that's when many get going. In fact, if many men and women were honest when they vowed their vows, they would rather love for better but not for worse, in health but not in sickness, for richer but not for poorer. But God asks us to love with a persevering love.

Before my parents married, my dad told my mom that if they were to be married, she would need to strike one word from her vocabulary: *divorce*. Giving up wasn't to be an option. Today, nearly fifty years later, it's clear that they've both taken that conversation and their vows seriously.

I urge you to strike the word *divorce* from your vocabulary also. But don't stop there. Mentally or emotionally checking out, coasting, avoiding, coexisting—none of these should be options either. Fight for your marriage every day. Fight against apathy. Fight against taking one another for granted. Fight against the slow erosion of friendship.

What better gift could you give to your future son or daughter than a marriage that will persevere? And not just persevere in name only, but persevere with heart and vigor and soul. As you lean on God for His empowering strength and as you keep your vows first unto Him, He will give you what you need to persevere in love.

Almost anyone can muster enough goodwill for an act of charity, even an extraordinary act of charity, from time to time. But continuing to show love when conditions are difficult—that is when love gets hard. What kind of empowerment do we have for this task?

_____

_____

_____

_____

_____

_____

_____

What will it mean for your children to grow up with the security of knowing their parents don't consider divorce an option?

_____

_____

_____

_____

_____

_____

_____

What Endures

*Love never fails. But where there are
prophecies, they will cease; where there
are tongues, they will be stilled; where
there is knowledge, it will pass away.*

1 CORINTHIANS 13:8

As we wrap up this devotional series on strengthening our marriages before Baby arrives, here's one final motivator. In this passage Paul told us that of all the spiritual gifts one could strive to have (1 Corinthians 12), love is one of the few that will endure into eternity. Prophecy, tongues, and knowledge, he wrote, will pass away, but love will remain.

When you cooperate with the Holy Spirit to strengthen your love for your spouse, you are working on something of eternal significance. Love is a change agent. As you love, *you* are being changed—changed into the likeness of God. As you love your spouse well, he is also being changed. Love's ripples go wide. Those who love well will bless their children and even great-great-grandchildren through their love. Those who love well will be a light to their neighbors and coworkers. These are things with eternal ramifications. But even more so, love is the business of eternity. In heaven we will have no need for prophecy or tongues, and what we thought we knew will seem but a dim picture. But we will go on loving for all eternity, loving God and our neighbors. Loving well, it seems, is one of the most significant things we can do with the days given to us.

Love is a muscle. The more you exercise it, the stronger it gets. Review what we've read about love in 1 Corinthians 13 by reading back through the entire Scripture passage. Write some specific things you can do to strengthen your love muscle—and your marriage—in the months to come.

_____

_____

_____

_____

_____

_____

_____

How will you make your marriage a priority in the face of the many challenges child rearing brings (sleeplessness, disagreements over discipline or training, lack of time alone, etc.)? How will your children see that, next to loving God, loving your husband is your top priority?

_____

_____

_____

_____

_____

_____

WEEK 24

The Wonder Within

The interaction between outside and inside the womb continues this week in that now your baby will not just hear sudden loud noises, but he or she will also blink repeatedly because of them. And others can feel baby moving if they place a well-timed and well-positioned hand to your belly. There's much less room now for doing cartwheels and back-flips than there was a few weeks ago. After all, your little one is almost a foot long, roughly the size of an ear of corn, and weighs around 1.32 pounds, so your uterus is not quite the jungle gym it used to be. But that won't stop your little karate kid from practicing round kicks, chops, and spin moves anytime soon.

As for you, enjoy this special time of sharing the life growing within you with your spouse and other children, if you have them. Let them feel the baby's kicks and have the joy of reading, singing, or just talking with Baby. What a great opportunity this is for bonding together as a family and preparing for the arrival of your little one. It's also a wonderful time for praising God together for how He is at work, fearfully and wonderfully forming this new addition to your family. Enjoy these special days of transition and delight in the wonder that is growing within you.

Points for Prayer and Praise

- Praise God for the chance to include your spouse in feeling Baby's movements.
- Pray for your little one as he or she begins learning your voice. Pray also that one day your son or daughter will come to know and discern God's voice.
- Pray that you will never lose sight of the fact that God has entrusted a human soul to your care. May you always treat him or her with the dignity that someone made in the image of God deserves.

Mommy's Memory Verse

"I tell you the truth, anyone who has faith in me will do what I have been doing. He will do even greater things than these, because I am going to the Father."

John 14:12

A Human Soul

He will be filled with the Holy
Spirit even from birth.

LUKE 1:15

*F*rom the separation of tissue into distinct fingers to the emergence of dips and ridges along the brain matter, the intricacy and complexity of a baby's development in utero can leave us speechless. But of all the things that amaze us, perhaps nothing is more arresting than the fact that you are carrying a tiny human soul. While our bodies will eventually pass away, our souls endure forever if we know Christ as our Savior. While our hair color will change and our muscles and eyesight will eventually wither, our souls will never perish. You carry within your womb something *eternal*. That's difficult to wrap the mind around.

Amidst dirty diapers, spit-up, and drool, it's easy to lose sight of the fact that even the tiniest humans are indeed persons, created in the image of God and possessing a soul. Why does this matter? This fact alone should affect how we treat our children. When we think of them, we should always keep in mind that we are dealing with persons, with souls who will one day be accountable before the living God. Parenting is not simply a matter of training or programming. It's a matter of shepherding a heart toward God. And we are responsible to the living God for how we treat these precious ones He has entrusted to our care. A human soul is nothing to be taken lightly.

When you meditate on the fact that God has entrusted a human soul into your care, it could not be any clearer that this little one does not exist for your personal happiness or fulfillment. He or she was created to glorify God and enjoy Him forever. How should this make a difference in how you serve this little one?

_____

_____

_____

_____

_____

_____

_____

_____

Write a prayer for your baby to come to know Jesus.

_____

_____

_____

_____

_____

_____

_____

God Is Moving Still

"I tell you the truth, anyone who has faith in me will do what I have been doing. He will do even greater things than these, because I am going to the Father."

JOHN 14:12

*Y*ou've probably been feeling your baby's movements for about a month. The feelings have progressed from almost imperceptible flutters to real, honest-to-goodness, no-mistaking-it kicks. Perhaps too your spouse or older children have even gotten the thrill of feeling the baby. If not, be patient. Ultimately, it seems baby's favorite time to play hide-and-seek is when somebody has a hand on Mama's tummy.

While those movements start small, in no time they get bigger. And before you know it, you're watching that bowl of ice cream you placed on the shelf of your stomach bounce from the somersault happening inside you.

As I think about my baby's movement inside me, my mind goes to a praise song that I love. It talks of how God is still moving, how He has always moved through history, and how He will continue moving to the end of time. It reminds me that God has been at work throughout the epochs, even in the bleakest parts. His work hasn't stopped just because Jesus is no longer walking this soil. Christ told His disciples that "they will do even greater things than these." Imagine that: even greater works than Jesus?! God's work has not ceased. It continues today, and you and I can be part of advancing it.

In what ways have you seen God move in your lifetime? How do you hope to be a part of the continued advancement of His kingdom?

_____

_____

_____

_____

_____

_____

_____

_____

Who, besides you, has been able to feel the baby's movement?

_____

_____

_____

_____

_____

_____

_____

Knowing His Voice

"His sheep follow him because they know his voice. But they will never follow a stranger; in fact, they will run away from him because they do not recognize a stranger's voice."

JOHN 10:4–5

By around twenty-three or twenty-four weeks, Baby can hear sounds outside the womb. Sounds inside the womb are muffled, but usually a mother's voice carries better because it originates from within and is stronger, richer, and less distorted than outside sounds. Lower frequencies travel through water better than higher ones, so often a father's deep voice reaches the baby without problems. In fact, many studies have documented how newborns will actually turn toward a mother's or father's familiar voice showing preference for those voices above others.

In the book of John, Jesus said, "I am the good shepherd; I know my sheep and my sheep know me" (10:14). He emphasized, "My sheep listen to my voice; I know them, and they follow me" (10:27). What does this mean for us? How do we learn the voice of the Good Shepherd? Like the baby in utero, proximity matters. Staying close to God helps us to *hear* His voice. But spending time with Him helps us *learn* His voice. Spending time in His Word, getting to know Him, and dwelling on His character helps us distinguish the voice of God from others. His voice protects us from harm (10:8) and leads us to verdant pastures and still waters (Psalm 23).

Perhaps you memorized Psalm 23 as a child. Reread this famous psalm. What character qualities of God do you find in this passage? What peace of mind do these attributes bring you?

_____

_____

_____

_____

_____

_____

_____

Dear Little One,

While you are growing inside Mommy, I want to be sure you learn my voice. Some of the special stories, songs, and lullabies I hope to share with you are . . .

_____

_____

_____

_____

_____

_____

Ask of Me

*"Behold, I have done according to your words;
see, I have given you a wise and understanding
heart, so that there has not been anyone like you
before you, nor shall any like you arise after you."*

1 KINGS 3:12 NKJV

*I*n the well-loved story of Aladdin, a magical genie appears, and the hero of the story gets the opportunity for three wishes. Like most of us, if given the opportunity, Aladdin squanders his wishes. In the book of 1 Kings we are told the story of Solomon's rise to the throne and of his prayer. God is certainly no genie catering to whims and wishes, but in this case He did grant Solomon's prayer for a wise and discerning heart so that he may govern God's people with justice. God is especially pleased that Solomon did not ask for wealth, long life, or the death of his enemies. So God decides to make Solomon the wisest man who ever lived, and on top of it all, He also blesses him with untold riches and honor.

So here's my question for you: when you pray for your baby, what do you pray for? Are your prayers like the silly squandered wishes of Aladdin, or do you pray for lasting things? Solomon's prayer for wisdom wasn't for himself; it was so that he could govern the people of God. So when you pray for your little one, consider petitioning God for kingdom-sized and kingdom-shaped prayers—prayers that God will mightily bless others through your child and further advance His gospel through your son's or daughter's life.

Is there anything for which you currently need wisdom? James 1:5 tells us that God gives generously of wisdom if we will but ask. Write a prayer for wisdom where you need it most today.

_____

_____

_____

_____

_____

_____

Lift your eyes from your son's or daughter's personal health and happiness as well as your own. Write a prayer asking God to use your child to bless others. You can be specific or vague, depending on how God leads. Just make sure your prayer is about more than just your child, that it is about bringing about God's will for His people through your little one.

_____

_____

_____

_____

_____

_____

WEEK 25

The Wonder Within

This week your little one is about the size of a head of romaine lettuce, ranging from 13.6 to 14.8 inches long, and weighs about 1.46 pounds. Inside the womb, Baby is navigating a new world of sensations. Through the sense of touch, your little adventurer is exploring by grasping fingers, toes, and even the umbilical cord, turning the body, and pressing feet against you. Baby's ears are learning to recognize your voice and the sounds of his or her environment—the loud whoosh of your blood flow, the beat of your heart, the gurgles of your stomach. The eyes are already beginning to sense light and darkness. And the taste buds that developed as early as eight to ten weeks are getting some practice as he or she pulls amniotic fluid into the mouth. Until recently, scientists did not believe the sense of smell was active in the womb, but newer research suggests that smell receptors are activated as amniotic fluid passes through the nasal cavity.

While food may be smelling and tasting good to you these days, you may be enjoying it less if you are already beginning to host one of pregnancy's most unwelcome houseguests: heartburn. Pregnant women tend to experience more heartburn than normal for several reasons: first, the rate of digestion slows in order to make sure that your little one gets as much of the nutrients in your food as possible. Second, pregnancy hormones such as progesterone relax the valve that separates the stomach and the esophagus, making it more likely for gastric acids to rise up. And third, as your uterus begins to crowd your other organs, including your stomach, stomach acids have no place to go but up. Stave heartburn off at the pass by eating smaller, more frequent meals and by avoiding extra spicy or greasy foods. And for those times when you just can't pass up the spicy chicken enchiladas, keep a bottle of antacids on hand and stay upright for a few hours after eating.

POINTS FOR PRAYER AND PRAISE

- Praise God for His wisdom evident in the design of your body to nourish, sustain, and bring forth this tiny little life.
- Pray for your little one as his or her tastes develop. Pray also that God will give him or her a taste and hunger for Christ in the days to come.
- Pray for wisdom as you decide on which childbirth classes to take and for God's help as you begin to prepare for labor.

MOMMY'S MEMORY VERSE

Train a child in the way he should go, and when he is old he will not turn from it.

PROVERBS 22:6

Marathon Prep

Train a child in the way he should go, and
when he is old he will not turn from it.

PROVERBS 22:6

Childbirth classes—does the thought send shivers down your spine? Well don't let it. When my husband and I were preparing for the birth of our first son, we went overboard. We attended many weeks of classes on childbirth, we read books, and we even practiced relaxation techniques together at home at night. But you know what? I'm so glad we were overprepared, and if I could advise others, I'd say to be overprepared too. Childbirth is like a marathon. I was so grateful my husband was prepared to coach me through labor, grateful that we both had trained together and knew how we would work together when the big day arrived.

But if childbirth is worth training for, certainly the real marathon of parenting is worth preparing for as well. This marathon begins the day your first child is born, and perhaps we don't truly meet the finish line until our lives are through. How will you and your husband work together? How will you persevere as individuals as well as a couple? What is your strategy to help your children grow in the fear of the Lord? These are things worth thinking about, talking about, reading about, and praying about. So yes, please prepare—scratch that— overprepare for labor. But even more so, please overprepare for the marathon of parenting. A great place to start your training is together, on your knees.

Have you and your husband read any Christian books on parenting? If not, think about doing so. What conversations have you had about any upcoming parenting issues? What topics do you need to talk more about?

_____

_____

_____

_____

_____

_____

Have you looked into any childbirth classes? What is something else you could do to overprepare for the day you will finally meet your baby?

_____

_____

_____

_____

_____

_____

_____

Growing Pains

*No discipline seems pleasant at the time,
but painful. Later on, however, it produces
a harvest of righteousness and peace for
those who have been trained by it.*

HEBREWS 12:11

*T*he day is winding down, and you find yourself with a stabbing pain in your lower abdomen. Or that normally comfy couch now has your back screaming. Or your stomach seems like it will never quit itching. And (gasp!) what are those lines? Pregnancy has its share of woes: round ligament pain, back and joint aches, itchy skin and stretch marks, not to mention frequent heartburn and constipation. If you've yet to experience these, sadly, it's probably just a matter of time. But all of these painful and uncomfortable experiences point to one thing: your body is producing something beautiful, something so very beautiful, and it is stretching the very fiber of your being.

When the Spirit of God works inside us, something similar happens. To produce spiritual fruit, God may bring trials. He may batter our selfish tendencies by bringing someone into our lives who has absolute need of us. He may break our self-reliance by bringing something too big for us to handle on our own. He may stretch our hearts by presenting us with a need that we are able to fill, but not without much sacrifice. God's spiritual work in us is stretching, pulling, sometimes even demolishing and rebuilding, but all of it is producing something so extraordinarily beautiful that even the angels bend low to see it (1 Peter 1:12).

In what areas of your life has God been stretching you? How has God used painful things in your recent past to produce spiritual fruit that will manifest in the future?

_____

_____

_____

_____

_____

_____

Athletes often call the training they undergo discipline. Whether it's learning a new instrument or perfecting a tennis serve, nothing comes to us without the disciplines that shape our abilities. Tell your little one about something you learned that took a lot of discipline. How was the experience painful at the time, but worth it in the end?

_____

_____

_____

_____

_____

_____

Shine the Light

God, who said, "Let light shine out of
darkness," made his light shine in our
hearts to give us the light of the knowledge
of the glory of God in the face of Christ.

2 CORINTHIANS 4:6

*Y*our baby is growing by leaps and bounds, weighing in now at almost 2 pounds. The brain has been steadily developing too, enabling him or her to respond to stimuli of the senses. In fact, if you were to shine a sharp light at your tummy, you might just get a jab in the rib cage.

Up until recently your baby had only known darkness. Similarly, until Christ apprehended us, our hearts were shrouded in darkness. Imagine for a moment being present at the creation of light. How stunning that first glimpse of light must have been! Likewise, in 2 Corinthians 4:6, Paul pointed out that the moment God illuminated our hearts, it was every bit as miraculous as the moment He first created light and summoned it to pierce the darkness.

How should we respond to this miracle? First, thinking on our redemption should continually compel us to praise God. Second, it calls us to "walk in the light, as he is in the light" (1 John 1:7). And finally, we respond by being beacons of His light: sharing our food with the hungry, clothing the poor, and not turning away from the hurting. When we do this, God promises His light will shine through us like the dawn, illuminating even more hearts as a result (Isaiah 58:7–9).

Take a few moments, close your eyes, and try to imagine creation's very first sunrise. Describe what you think it would have been like to see this miracle. As you reflect on the beauty of light, praise God for what it tells us about who He is and how He calls us to live.

_____

_____

_____

_____

_____

_____

_____

Tell your little one about a time when God used you to shine His light toward someone else (see Isaiah 58:6–7 for examples).

_____

_____

_____

_____

_____

_____

_____

Savoring God

Taste and see that the LORD is good; blessed
is the man who takes refuge in him.

PSALM 34:8

*W*ill your little one like broccoli or turnip greens? Believe it or not, your baby's tastes are already being formed. Amniotic fluid, which carries the tastes and smells of a mother's food, is constantly surrounding the nose and tongue of your little one.

We all know that, for better or worse, we influence the tastes of our children. Most of us just didn't know that the influence begins even in utero. By the time they are toddling about, they are taking note of us—picking up our penchant for sweets or mimicking the way we munch on healthy foods such as carrots and grapes.

But even more importantly, whether we know it or not, we will influence their spiritual tastes. Will we whet their appetite for more of God? Or will we leave them with nothing but a bitter predisposition to spiritual things? In large part, it depends not on what we say but on what we savor.

In Psalm 34:8 David bid others to try for themselves and experience the goodness of the Lord. Elsewhere, we see how David savored the sweetness of God's laws (Psalm 19:10); in fact, he compared them to honey. Do you crave the sweetness of fellowship with God? Do you meditate on His laws, relishing their goodness? May your child become a connoisseur of the richest fare because of you.

Does it seem foreign to you to describe the law of God with words like sweet *and* honey *(Psalm 19:10)? How are the laws of God sweet to you?*

_____

_____

_____

_____

_____

_____

_____

Tell your little one about a particularly sweet time of fellowship you once had with God. Pray for him or her to come to hunger and thirst for God and His righteousness (Matthew 5:6).

_____

_____

_____

_____

_____

_____

_____

WEEK 26

The Wonder Within

*I*nside the womb, God continues to be at work fearfully and wonderfully fashioning the mind and body of your little wonder. He or she now weighs around 1.7 pounds and stretches to between 13.6 and 14.8 inches long (still about the length of a head of romaine lettuce). God's intricacy is more visible in your baby's spine—already composed of 150 joints, 33 rings, and around 1,000 ligaments. A network of capillaries, filled with blood, now give your little one—whose skin is mostly transparent—a reddish hue. Meanwhile, your baby's hair, which has lacked pigment up to this point, is now taking on the color and texture you will see at birth. Lungs have begun producing surfactant, a key development in the ability to survive outside of the womb.

While Baby is practicing breathing, you may be breathing a bit easier too, as most babies born after twenty-six weeks survive. While your baby's birth day is ultimately in God's hands, you still hold the responsibility of caring for your body and your baby in such a way as to promote his or her best chances of a full-term delivery. Believe it or not, one thing you can do that will help is to take care of your teeth and gums. Oddly enough, severe gum disease can lead to periodontitis, a condition that has been linked to both premature birth and preeclampsia (high blood pressure and excess protein). So, for your little buddy's sake, make sure flossing and a dental checkup are on your mommy "to do" list.

Points for Prayer and Praise

🍼 Praise God that you have reached this point in pregnancy when most infants born prematurely survive with medical care.

🍼 Pray for your little one's spinal development. Pray also that your son or daughter will one day have the spiritual backbone to stand up for what is right.

🍼 Pray that God will provide you with good friends as you complete this leg of pregnancy and approach the upcoming trimester of your journey. Ask that they will be wise counselors and strong encouragers, especially as this road reaches its destination.

Mommy's Memory Verse

Plans fail for lack of counsel, but with many advisers they succeed. A man finds joy in giving an apt reply—and how good is a timely word!

Proverbs 15:22–23

Craving Christ

"Blessed are those who hunger and thirst
for righteousness, for they will be filled."

MATTHEW 5:6

The first trimester it was apples; the second, avocados; and now as I write this in my third trimester, I've had my taste buds set on artichokes. Cravings are crazy and often bizarre.

So what do our cravings mean? Sometimes they mean nothing. Other times they may indicate a deficiency. For example, if you find yourself craving ice, you may actually have an iron deficiency. If you're craving steak, oranges, or a handful of nuts, it doesn't hurt to give your body what it wants; perhaps you are in need of protein, vitamin C, or some healthy fats. Other cravings, like my nonstop-Chick-fil-A-cookies-and-cream-milkshake craving, are probably fine to indulge in once in a while, but most of the time should be redirected to healthier options, like a glass of milk or a cup of yogurt.

Jesus talked about cravings of a spiritual kind in the Beatitudes. Blessed, He said, are those who hunger and thirst after righteousness, for they will be filled. Like those deficient in key vitamins and minerals, those who hunger after righteousness realize that they are needy and desperate. Christ loves to satisfy those who can plainly see their emptiness and who know that nothing but more of Him can satisfy.

Why is righteousness something we should crave?

_____

_____

_____

_____

_____

_____

_____

_____

Tell your little one about any cravings you may have already
experienced.

_____

_____

_____

_____

_____

_____

_____

Friends for the Journey

*Plans fail for lack of counsel, but with
many advisers they succeed. A man
finds joy in giving an apt reply—
and how good is a timely word!*

PROVERBS 15:22–23

Several months before our first son's arrival, I tucked my pregnant belly under the table as my husband and I sat down to supper. Before we prayed, I asked, "Honey, can you pray that God will help me begin forming deeper friendships with godly moms?" My husband looked surprised. He knew I already had good friends. But I knew that one season of my life was closing and another season was beginning. I would need some good friends for this new leg of my journey. I also knew that being at home full-time would mean my world of adult interaction would be shrinking. Cultivating friendships with women in the same life stage would be healthy both for me and my marriage; it wouldn't be fair to put the full weight of my relational needs on my husband.

I'm so grateful that God answered those prayers. Having such friendships meant having someone to ask for advice when my ten-month-old was still waking up five times a night, or hearing a reassuring voice when my baby hit a milestone later than normal, or when I felt like throwing in the pee-soaked towel on toilet training. How good it is to have many advisers! How reassuring it is to hear that "apt reply" at the moment you desperately need it.

Do you have godly mommy friends to walk this next leg of the journey with you? If not, don't worry. Just begin praying. God will supply your needs. Write a prayer here for God to bring the right people into your life and to deepen the relationships you already have.

_____

_____

_____

_____

_____

_____

The friends your child makes will be one of the most determinative life influences. Write a prayer for God to bless your child with the right friends at the right times. Ask God specifically for friends who will influence your child to pursue Him more deeply.

_____

_____

_____

_____

_____

_____

Unspoken Fears

Do not fear what they fear, and do not dread it. The Lord Almighty is the one you are to regard as holy, he is the one you are to fear.

ISAIAH 8:12–13

*H*as your dream life taken on a life of its own lately? If so, you're not alone. Ask just about any woman who's been pregnant before and she'll likely remember those strange and vivid dreams of pregnancy. As mentioned earlier, there is a biological basis for this uptick in memorable and often bizarre dreams. Although pregnant women have less REM sleep—the kind in which dreams occur—they are more likely to remember their dreams due to more frequent night-wakings.

For many, pregnancy dreams can be disturbing. A few I remember from my first pregnancy: forgetting to feed the baby for over twenty-four hours and losing my walking toddler in sinking mud. Others report dreaming about a husband being unfaithful. Dreams like these betray our worst fears: inadequacy in motherhood, disaster befalling our little ones, or the unraveling of our marriage.

You've undoubtedly heard the oft-quoted words of Franklin Roosevelt, "The only thing we have to fear is fear itself."[3] But more accurately, the Bible tells us that the only thing we have to fear is God Himself. Again and again, the Bible tells us to fear—to treat with awe and reverence—the Lord. And again and again, the Bible tells us not to be afraid of what others fear. Christ's sufficiency and His grace answer and calm every fear we have. With Him, we face nothing alone, and nothing without His empowerment.

In the book of Job, a God-fearing man faces every possible fear a man could face, and yet he was able to say, "The LORD gave and the LORD has taken away; may the name of the LORD be praised" (1:21). How does Christ enable us to face any fear with confidence?

_____

_____

_____

_____

_____

Have you had any dreams you think would be funny or sweet for your little one to know about one day? (It may be better not to record the scary ones!) If not, tell your little one about a dream you have for his or her life.

_____

_____

_____

_____

_____

_____

Forget-Me-Not

*Remember that you were slaves in Egypt
and the LORD your God redeemed you. That
is why I give you this command today.*

DEUTERONOMY 15:15

You were fifteen minutes late to your doctor's appointment because you couldn't find your keys. After the appointment you stood befuddled in the parking lot trying to remember where you parked, only to discover you'd come out the other side of the building. And on the way home, you drove right past your turn. If this is you lately, chalk it up to "pregnancy brain."

While our brains don't actually change during pregnancy, we do have between fifteen to forty times more progesterone and estrogen flooding our system, and studies have shown that the high volumes of these hormones can affect spatial memory (*Where are those keys?*). Plus, we may be multitasking, exhausted, or just have our minds on Baby. Whatever the case, we are prone to forgetfulness these days.

In Deuteronomy we see one word often repeated: *remember.* As the Israelites prepared to take the promised land, God was adamant that they remember Him and His works. One of my professors in seminary, Dr. Bruce Waltke—a translator of the NIV—used to say the opposite of *remember* is not *forget*; it is *dismember.* We forget who we are by disassociating from God and dismembering ourselves from the body of believers. We can learn to remember rightly when we join together with other believers and rehearse what God has done in our lives and in the Bible.

Write about a time of God's faithfulness to you in the past. Share this story with someone this week and ask them to share a story of their own. Notice how, as we remind each other of God's faithfulness, we remember God and who we are in Christ.

_____

_____

_____

_____

_____

_____

_____

_____

Have you had any episodes of "pregnancy brain" yet? Tell your little one about one or two of them.

_____

_____

_____

_____

_____

_____

_____

WEEK 27

The Wonder Within

So, what's your little one up to now? Nearly half of his or her energy is going to brain development these days. Your little Einstein-in-the-making is having a brain spurt! Around this time the brain weight increases between 400 and 500 percent. Meanwhile your little one is waking and sleeping at regular intervals, hiccuping, opening and closing the eyes, bulking up with fat, and strengthening his or her immune system. Baby may even be sucking on fingers or a thumb—a great way to practice for getting meals in the days to come. By the way, your little one isn't so little any more. Your bundle of wonder is weighing in at 1.93 pounds and in the range of 13.6 to 14.8 inches long—still about the size of a head of romaine lettuce.

As you near the end of your second trimester, you may be experiencing some new and unwanted pregnancy symptoms. Leg cramps at night, swelling in the hands, feet, and ankles, a return of fatigue, and perhaps even Braxton Hicks (practice contractions that feel like a brief tightening of the belly). While these are all uncomfortable, try to keep your mind on the prize ahead and on the privilege it is to house a human soul. And as friends and family begin to lend extra hands or send extra prayers, don't turn down their gracious offers! Accept them as God's grace to you in this season when you carry not just the weight of one life but two.

POINTS FOR PRAYER AND PRAISE

- Praise God for the people He has put in your life who desire to bless you and your baby, whether it be by throwing you a shower, offering advice, or passing along hand-me-downs.
- Pray for the continued development of your baby's brain. Pray also that one day your little one might possess not just knowledge but also godly wisdom, rooted in the fear of the Lord.
- Pray that you would remember the dignity and importance of the calling you have as mother and that you would exhibit a servant's heart before your children.

MOMMY'S MEMORY VERSE

"Instead, whoever wants to become great among you must be your servant."

MATTHEW 20:26

A Divine Calling

God blessed them and said to them,
"Be fruitful and increase in number;
fill the earth and subdue it."

GENESIS 1:28

*B*efore the fall, God called men and women to be fruitful and multiply. While this command certainly encompasses much more than physical offspring, it by no means belittles the importance of the most literal interpretation. Motherhood is a high and holy calling—given by God Himself. In fact, this calling was so important that it is included in the very first words God spoke to humankind. Mothering would be one of the ways in which Eve would fulfill the commands of God, one of the ways in which she would please her Creator.

After the fall, we see an even greater significance revealed in Eve's role of "mother of all the living" (Genesis 3:20). God revealed that salvation would come through the offspring of the woman (3:15). God could have brought the Messiah in many ways. But we take for granted that He chose to bring Him into the world in the most ordinary fashion, as a baby, through an earthly woman's womb. The King of kings, the Son of God, came to earth through something as seemingly undignified as childbirth. God calls women to motherhood not as some second-rate calling. Our calling—from carrying a child in the womb, to actually giving birth, to nurturing and raising that child up in the way of the Lord—is dignified from beginning to end by the God-ordained nature of it.

While God does not call every woman to bear children, He certainly has ordained motherhood as an important and significant aspect of His calling on the lives of many women. How does the divine nature of this calling, as well as Christ's own coming through a woman, communicate the dignity of your role as mother?

_____

_____

_____

_____

_____

_____

Mothering is spiritual work—a means by which we worship our Creator and bring Him honor. Write a prayer asking for God's help in this spiritual work that lies ahead of you.

_____

_____

_____

_____

_____

_____

A Holy Calling

"Go and make disciples of all nations, baptizing them in the name of the Father and of the Son and of the Holy Spirit, and teaching them to obey everything I have commanded you."

MATTHEW 28:19–20

In Genesis God called Adam and Eve and humankind after them to be fruitful and multiply—to fill the earth and subdue it (Genesis 1:28). This first command occupies a preeminent place in Scripture. But in the New Testament, if there were a corresponding command in terms of preeminence, without a doubt it will be the Great Commission. While many think of this passage as the great call to evangelism and missions (which it certainly is), it is also, just as importantly, a call to discipleship. And this is a call that certainly goes out to all Christian mothers.

One of the reasons mothering is a holy calling is because mothering is the nurturing of a human soul. As mothers, we do everything within our power to woo our children with the hope and beauty of the gospel and the person of Christ. And we labor to see our children become more Christlike and more submitted to Christ in every arena of their lives—this is the core of discipleship. As we do this with the infinitely important souls entrusted to our keeping, we are participating in the heart and soul of the Great Commission, doing *the* most important work Jesus left us to do.

The Great Commission instructs us to teach others to obey all that Jesus has commanded. How does this verse amplify your view of motherhood and the dignity of your work?

_____

_____

_____

_____

_____

The most important thing you will ever give your children is not an Ivy League education, exposure to music or the arts, fun family vacations, or all the comforts money can buy. The most important thing you will ever give your children is a winsome exposure to the gospel through your words, your actions, and your ongoing discipleship relationship with them. When you search your heart, does it reflect these kinds of priorities?

_____

_____

_____

_____

_____

High Hopes

"Instead, whoever wants to become great among you must be your servant."

MATTHEW 20:26

*E*very mother wants the best for her children. From even before she holds that baby in her arms, she's already hoping great things for the life of that someday man or woman. The mother of James and John, two of Christ's disciples, was no different. As an early follower of Christ, she knew that the best for them could only be found in Christ. So she asked Jesus, "Grant that one of these two sons of mine may sit at your right and the other at your left in your kingdom" (Matthew 20:21).

This mother envisioned greatness for her two sons, perhaps a seat of honor and power, and most likely an earthly kingdom. When Christ replied to her question with a question, "Can you drink the cup I am going to drink?" the sons replied, "We can," showing they had no idea what their request entailed (20:22). To drink from Christ's cup meant to share in His sufferings. To sit near Him meant, not power, but meekness and servanthood. To be first meant to be last.

The ironic lesson here is that if we truly desire greatness for our children, we must help them obtain it by modeling the heart of a servant. In God's kingdom a leader leads by taking up the basin and the towel and washing another's feet. This is the way of His upside-down kingdom. The only way up is down.

Sometimes our dreams for our children do not align with God's dreams. One mother dreamed of greatness and power for her sons when true greatness means serving, not being served. What dreams for our children should we submit to Christ? How can we make this both a habit and a posture?

_____

_____

_____

_____

_____

_____

_____

Motherhood is by nature a journey into servanthood and sacrifice. Write a prayer asking for God to help you serve joyfully and as unto Him.

_____

_____

_____

_____

_____

_____

Emptying Self

Your attitude should be the same as that
of Christ Jesus: Who . . . made himself
nothing, taking the very nature of a
servant, being made in human likeness.

PHILIPPIANS 2:5–7

If there is one thing certain about motherhood, it is this: sacrifice. Pregnancy is just a prelude. We endure morning sickness, aversions, aches, sleeplessness, and finally labor. We deny ourselves a venti latte, a sushi roll, or an Advil. This is just a small foretaste of the sacrifices we will make as mothers: from those first sleepless nights to the niceties we give up to send our children to college. While such sacrifices are not without joy, they are sacrifices nonetheless, and our days are full of them.

In Philippians 2 we have what is likely one of the oldest hymns of the church. In this moving poetic passage, we are reminded of how Christ did not grasp after God's power, but instead took a servant's form and allowed Himself to be made in the most fragile and vulnerable of human forms—a newborn baby. From His humble beginnings to the height of His ministry to His death on the cross, He exemplified a servant's heart. And He gave us a model for how we too should minister in our holy calling as mothers. As we sacrifice for our little ones, we can imitate Christ in our daily lives. We worship Him by doing even the most menial acts unto God and for His glory.

Christ gave up the comforts of heaven to come to earth as a baby and die as an ordinary scoundrel on a cross outside of Jerusalem. Is there anything God has asked you to give up in order to be the mother He wants you to be? What other sacrifices do you see ahead?

_____

_____

_____

_____

_____

_____

_____

In Hebrews 12:2 we learn that Christ endured the cross "for the joy set before him." What joys gleam on the horizon as future motivators for the daily sacrifices motherhood requires? Which of these joys are temporal and which are eternal?

_____

_____

_____

_____

_____

_____

YOUR COMING WONDER:

Third Trimester

WEEK 28

The Wonder Within

You made it to your final trimester! You and your little one have both come a long way. Remember that poppy seed–sized wonder you began getting to know when you found out you were pregnant? Well, now he or she weighs about 2.22 pounds and is somewhere between 13.6 and 14.8 inches long (still about the length of a head of romaine lettuce)! This week your baby's sleep patterns begin following circadian rhythms. That means you will notice more regular patterns of sleep. When your little one's eyes are open, he or she may be practicing blinking now. And if you could peer within the womb you'd see that those eyes now have a pigment—though they may still change color in the months to come (eyes don't assume their permanent shade until about nine months after birth).

You've come a long way too, Mama! You've gone from hardly showing to looking like a pumpkin smuggler. The average woman has gained between 18 and 25 pounds by now and will gain about 11 pounds in her final trimester. Your weight-gain needs may be above or below these numbers depending on your starting weight and BMI (body mass index). As the final trimester gets started, fix your eyes firmly on Christ to see you through the discomforts and labor ahead. But also remember the miracle of the growing life within you. Holding this sweet little one in your arms will make every discomfort you've borne so worth it.

Points for Prayer and Praise

🍼 Praise God for helping you reach the third and final trimester of your pregnancy.

🍼 Pray for your little one to continue thriving, and to continue letting you know through daily kick (or fetal movement) counts (something your health-care provider will likely advise you to do in the coming months). Also pray that as your little one grows, he or she may thrive spiritually, knowing the abundant life that is only available through Christ.

🍼 Pray for yourself as you undergo the glucose screening test, most likely sometime this week. Pray for a healthy report if it is the Lord's will.

Mommy's Memory Verse

Since we are surrounded by such a great cloud of witnesses, let us throw off everything that hinders and the sin that so easily entangles, and let us run with perseverance the race marked out for us.

Hebrews 12:1

Date:

Finishing Well

*Since we are surrounded by such a
great cloud of witnesses, let us throw off
everything that hinders and the sin that
so easily entangles, and let us run with
perseverance the race marked out for us.*

HEBREWS 12:1

*C*ongratulations! You have completed your second trimester and the finish line is firmly in sight. You've made it through the trials of morning sickness and aversions to food and smells. You've shared the news with friends and likely seen your little wonder through the miracle of ultrasound. But there's still the most important part of the race to come. For many, the third trimester is the hardest. As you and Baby continue to grow, so does your discomfort. Night wakings, backaches, heartburn, fears about labor: the last few miles can be the hardest. You need grace to finish well.

In Hebrews 11 the author pointed out those who finished well because they finished full of faith. They were people who, like Abraham, did not receive the fullness of the promises God had made to them in their lifetime, but could look to their faithful God to fulfill His Word within the realm of eternity (Hebrews 11:13, 16). Faith looks forward with a trust based firmly in the character of God.

As you enter into the last leg of this pregnancy journey, look forward with faith and remember the character of your faithful God. Not only will He help you run the larger race of your Christian journey, He will also help you finish this pregnancy well as you look to Him for strength and grace.

List some of the attributes of God. As you reflect on who He is, how does it increase your faith and your ability to trust Him for the unseen?

_____

_____

_____

_____

_____

_____

What have been some of the highlights of your pregnancy journey so far? Praise God for these moments and ask Him for His grace and help to finish well.

_____

_____

_____

_____

_____

_____

Leaving Glory

[Jesus] made Himself of no reputation,
taking the form of a bondservant,
and coming in the likeness of men.

PHILIPPIANS 2:7 NKJV

*M*aybe it's because my son is due so near Christmas, but I find myself often thinking about Mary and her pregnancy journey. She was so young, and yet she was given such an enormous privilege and responsibility. As my mind wanders to Mary, I wonder again at how Christ could step away from His glory and the heavenly realms and take on flesh. Even beyond that, He took the form of a baby—the most vulnerable and dependent form He could have taken. What did it mean for the enormity of deity—of omnipotence, omniscience, and eternality—to shrink to the form of a tiny baby? What did it mean for Christ to lower Himself to take on the mantle of humanity?

Christ who stepped away from it all, Christ who emptied Himself, Christ who stooped to serve—this Christ is to be our model. This is the One whom we emulate. This is the One whom we seek to pattern our lives after. As you embrace the call of mothering your new little one, are you stepping away from some places of honor—perhaps a job where your work was valued? Will you be putting a degree on the shelf for a while, or will a talent lie dormant while you turn your attention to diapers and spit-up? If so, you are following in good footsteps; Christ left it all to serve.

Spend some time meditating on Christ becoming a human baby. How does the way He came amplify your desire to worship Him? What amazes you about the incarnation?

_____

_____

_____

_____

_____

_____

_____

It was very important to God that Christ be able to identify with us in every way—in vulnerability, in weakness, in hunger and thirst, in hardship, and in pain. Write a prayer for your future son or daughter that he or she would turn to Christ as the One who can relate to our every struggle.

_____

_____

_____

_____

_____

_____

_____

Give Up to Gain

"When you fast, do not look somber as the hypocrites do, for they disfigure their faces to show men they are fasting. I tell you the truth, they have received their reward in full."

MATTHEW 6:16

It's a lot like drinking Kool-Aid. If you've been pregnant before, you remember the orange sugary drink you'll soon be asked to chugalug for your glucose screening test. This common screening test checks to see how efficiently your body processes sugar in order to see if you might be at risk for gestational diabetes, a condition that affects 2 to 5 percent of pregnant women. Depending on your doctor or midwife, you may be asked to fast for this test. And fasting when you're twenty-four weeks pregnant can seem like a Herculean effort! After all, housing two means twice the rumbly tummy.

In general, fasting isn't advised in pregnancy. But if we look at Jesus' example, we know that fasting is good for our spiritual health. In fact, in this passage in Matthew we see that Jesus expected His people would fast. So here's an idea: fasting doesn't have to involve abstaining from food. Pick a day, week, or weekend and abstain from your various technological devices. When you unplug, you'll be surprised how much extra time you have to recharge with God. Seek His face on behalf of this child you are carrying. Pray that this little one will one day come to Christ. And pray over your own example as you mother this child.

Fasting isn't simply abstaining from something. It is using that abstinence as a way to spur yourself to refocus your attention on God. What other things besides food and technology might you be able to abstain from in order to refocus your attention on God?

_____

_____

_____

_____

_____

_____

Make a plan. How can you make a time for fasting (from something besides physical nourishment, which your baby needs) and prayer before this little one comes?

_____

_____

_____

_____

_____

_____

Date:

Catalyst to Wonder

*When I consider your heavens, the work
of your fingers, the moon and the stars,
which you have set in place, what is
man that you are mindful of him, the
son of man that you care for him?*

PSALM 8:3–4

*M*ove over, Radio City Music Hall! Your little one is putting the Rockettes to shame. There's a whole lot of kicking going on, isn't there? Now's a great time to begin tuning in to your little Rockette's movements. Your health-care provider will likely instruct you soon to take some time out each day when your baby is most active and make a record of how long it takes to feel ten fetal movements. You should feel ten movements within about an hour. If you don't, try lying down or getting a fruit drink or snack to perk your little kicker up a bit. Kick counts (or as some health-care providers call them, fetal movement counts) are used as a way to monitor your baby's well-being in the womb and to help ensure that, should there be any drastic cessation of movement for twenty-four hours, a mother consults her practitioner.

But kick counts are also a perfect time to tune in to the wonder of pregnancy and God's work within you. The psalmist considered the vast expanse of the night sky and wondered, *What is man that God is mindful of him?* As you place your hands on your tummy, consider this work within you, a work of His fingers surely more dazzling than any starry night. Let the wonder of this life within dazzle you again.

Let those tiny—and sometimes big—kicks be a catalyst to turn your thoughts to Him again in worship. God has chosen you to be a mother to this particular child. What a wonder; what a joy! Praise Him!

Consider the pure wonder of God creating a life within you. Describe your thoughts as you contemplate this miracle.

_____

_____

_____

_____

_____

_____

When is your little one most active? Imagine you are telling your son or daughter one day about what it felt like to feel him or her kick. Describe it here in the best detail you can.

_____

_____

_____

_____

_____

_____

WEEK 29

The Wonder Within

*Y*our little wonder is getting in a lot of practice in these remaining months before his or her world debut. About 30 to 40 percent of the time, Baby is practicing breathing. One by-product of that is the strange repetitive thumping you may feel from time to time. Nope, they're not kicks, but rather, baby hiccups! Don't worry; they don't disturb baby. (No one knows definitively why fetal hiccuping occurs, but it is likely because a small amount of amniotic fluid is pulled into the lungs during Baby's practice breathing sessions and the diaphragm contracts to try to expel it.) Your little one continues filling out, looking a lot less wrinkly at a whopping 2.5 pounds and somewhere between 15.2 and 16.7 inches long (about the length of a pineapple). From here on out, Baby will gain about a half pound each week until birth.

How about you? Are you feeling occasionally breathless? That's because the top of your uterus, now 3 inches above your belly button, is pushing into your ribs and diaphragm. That crowding may also be causing heartburn. And you can blame your limited internal real estate once again for why you're running to the bathroom so much; the weight of Baby is squishing your bladder into oblivion. Take heart, though; God has designed your baby and your body perfectly. Though it may feel like there's no room for either of you to grow anymore, God has it under control. By the time Baby has outgrown this temporary home, you will be holding him or her in your arms.

POINTS FOR PRAYER AND PRAISE

- Praise God for the opportunity you have to disciple your child and to raise him or her up in the way of the Lord.
- Pray for your little one as his or her brain begins to regulate body temperature. Pray also that, as your son or daughter grows up, he or she would not be lukewarm about the things of God, but rather have a heart aflame with passion for Him.
- Pray for yourself that God would help you not to compare yourself or your child to others and that He would give you a heart of contentment and gratitude.

MOMMY'S MEMORY VERSE

The LORD your God is with you, he is mighty to save. He will take great delight in you, he will quiet you with his love, he will rejoice over you with singing.

ZEPHANIAH 3:17

Wisdom's Design

O LORD, how manifold are Your works!
In wisdom You have made them all.

PSALM 104:24 NKJV

*D*oes the couch that used to feel so nice to relax on now make your back ache? Don't worry; it's not old age creeping up on you. You can thank the pregnancy hormone relaxin for getting in the way of your relaxing. While you may be cursing that hormone now, you'll be thankful for it in a few months when it comes time to push. Relaxin's job is to—as its name implies—relax your joints, ligaments, and muscles in preparation for both housing your growing baby and going through labor. Your pelvis and lower back are actually flexing for this miraculous feat ahead.

God's creation of our bodies is truly amazing. He orchestrates hormones, muscles, ligaments, and joints, not to mention the creation of a life that is slowly taking shape from a single fertilized egg. Have you stopped lately to marvel at God's handiwork? There is wisdom in His creation down to the smallest cellular or hormonal level. And whether you see it or not, there is wisdom in the unfolding of His providence in your life, from the timing of this child to the exact number of days He has granted you. There is wisdom in the minutiae of every facet of your life.

Take some time to stop and notice the wisdom of God manifest in His creation. Enjoy Him and praise Him through His handiwork.

Be still and marvel at some aspect of God's wisdom made manifest in His creations. Write your thoughts and praise here.

_____

_____

_____

_____

_____

_____

_____

One day this baby you are carrying will be a curious preschooler, asking "why" questions and stopping to examine rocks and bugs. You can see these questions and pauses either as a nuisance or as a chance to slow down and be amazed at God's creation. Write a prayer for yourself that God might use your child to renew your childlike wonder of who He is and what He has made.

_____

_____

_____

_____

_____

_____

_____

Rejoicing over You

The LORD your God is with you, he is
mighty to save. He will take great delight
in you, he will quiet you with his love,
he will rejoice over you with singing.

ZEPHANIAH 3:17

Streamers, games, cake, and presents—baby showers are so much fun! Perhaps some friends or coworkers of yours are already starting to plan one for you. If so, don't take such a shower of love for granted. You are deeply blessed to have people who care so much. Or perhaps you're feeling a bit overlooked because there's no one around who's asking to plan such a special time for you. If so, I want to encourage you now. You are not alone, and you and the life you are carrying are absolutely precious and are being celebrated by God Himself.

The prophet Zephaniah wrote that God takes great delight in His people. When His people return to Him in repentance, He rejoices over them with singing. Similarly, in Isaiah 62:5 we find that "as a bridegroom rejoices over his bride, so will your God rejoice over you." If you are a child of His, God is delighting over you, rejoicing over you with singing. We all know how good it feels to be showered with the love and attention of friends and family. How much better it is to be showered by the love and attention of the Creator of all! Stop and take it in for a moment. He delights in you.

So many of us struggle with issues of self-worth and self-confidence. Sometimes that struggle can be debilitating. How does it affect you to really meditate on God delighting in you? Can you picture God singing over you?

_____

_____

_____

_____

_____

_____

When you finally hold your little one in your arms, you will know in a very deep way what it is to delight in someone. Perhaps you'll even sing over him or her with lullabies as you rock that little one to sleep. As your son or daughter grows, how will you continue to let your child know that you delight in him or her?

_____

_____

_____

_____

_____

_____

Sympathy Symptoms

*Carry each other's burdens, and in this
way you will fulfill the law of Christ.*

GALATIANS 6:2

*H*as your husband been putting on a little weight around the middle?
Perhaps he's got a few cravings of his own, or maybe he's downing the
antacids faster than you are. Well, if so, there is actually a name for
these sympathy symptoms. It's called couvade syndrome, and believe it
or not, it's common. Some researchers call it psychosomatic; others say
there's a physiological root. In fact, they've found that men's testosterone, estradiol, prolactin, and cortisol levels change when they're living
in close contact with a pregnant woman. Go figure.

Whatever is really going on, it's nice to have someone who understands, at least on some level, what you are going through. Offering
sympathy or in some cases, empathy is a way we show compassion. But
often we can take it a step further: when we see a brother or sister in
need, we can actually offer to carry some of the burden ourselves. We
can make a meal for the friend recovering from surgery. We can offer
to babysit the children for the mom who is frazzled and sleep deprived.
And we can share a cup of tea with the widow whose burden is loneliness. As we minister, we remember and imitate Christ who went the full
distance: carrying the weight of our sin and guilt to the cross and suffering in our place. He carried our burden so that our own yoke might
be light.

Is there an opportunity around you to carry someone else's burden? What is it? Brainstorm here a few ways in which perhaps you could help.

_____

_____

_____

_____

_____

In order to share our children's burdens, we need to hear their hearts. Sometimes simple practices give children the opportunity to unload. Maybe it's going on a nightly walk, having dinner together, or even sharing a chore like washing dishes together. What rhythms do you want to include in your family life to provide moments for heart-to-heart sharing?

_____

_____

_____

_____

_____

_____

Measuring Up

*A heart at peace gives life to the
body, but envy rots the bones.*

PROVERBS 14:30

*T*rust me, we've all done it. You catch a sidelong view of a friend or coworker who is due around the same time as you and quickly make an assessment. "Man, why do I look so much bigger than her?" Or you quietly pat yourself on the back because another woman looks twice as big as you. As women we are always comparing ourselves. When it comes to pregnancy, we all carry weight differently, and our weight gain or even the way we carry our babies may vary from pregnancy to pregnancy. But still we seem to have a compulsion to see how we stack up.

And it doesn't stop there. Once the babies are born, we compare how quickly or slowly we lose the baby weight. And we also compare our babies: their size, when they reach certain milestones, their temperaments, even their looks. Then, depending on our assessment of how we and our little ones measure up, we are tempted toward either pride or envy.

Why do we put ourselves through this kind of torture—always measuring ourselves and our children? When we instead find our identity and value in Jesus Christ, we are saved so much heartache and so much misplaced energy. A heart at peace enables us to experience the fullness of life, but comparisons either result in envy that rots us from the inside out and turns even some of our best moments (pregnancy, early motherhood) bitter with disappointment or gives us false security.

The only measurement that truly matters is our righteousness in Christ. And the Bible is quite clear that all have sinned and fallen short of the glory of God. This is why Christ came and died, so that we would be covered in His righteousness. Write a prayer of repentance for comparing yourself to others in the first place and of thanks that you don't have to find your value in how you measure up to others.

_____

_____

_____

_____

_____

_____

What are some ways you can avoid falling into the comparison trap, especially as you grow bigger in the months ahead and after your little one has arrived?

_____

_____

_____

_____

_____

_____

_____

WEEK 30

The Wonder Within

Your little one just keeps on growing. This week Baby is weighing in at 2.9 pounds and stretching between 15.2 and 16.7 inches long. Last week the brain began to regulate breathing activity and temperature. And now Baby can start shedding lanugo, that fine covering of hair that had been in place to help keep him or her warm. As more neural connections are made, the brain continues to fold and crease, increasing the surface area of the brain's cortical area. That's a sign that your little one is gaining intelligence (creatures less complex than humans have smaller and smoother brains). While the total surface area of the brain of any given adult is the same, the size of various areas of the brain differs from person to person. That may result in our unique abilities and capacities.

While your baby continues to grow smarter, you may be feeling a little more fuzzy-headed. Don't worry; you aren't actually losing brain cells. Research has been able to show that pregnancy hormones only play an affect on spatial memory, so if you're having difficulty remembering where you put your cell phone or keys, chalk it up to the so-called pregnancy brain. Otherwise, if your memory feels fuzzy, it might just be due to lack of sleep or a change in your priorities with Baby's arrival on the horizon.

POINTS FOR PRAYER AND PRAISE

- Praise God for this time He has given you to prepare your heart and mind for being a mother to this little one.
- Pray for the unique development of your baby's brain. Pray that, as he or she grows and identifies the unique gifts and abilities God has given, your son or daughter will use those skills to God's glory.
- Pray for help in all the decisions you will make in the last trimester—from decisions about birth to choices about which pediatrician to choose. Pray for wisdom and peace.

MOMMY'S MEMORY VERSE

I have been reminded of your sincere faith, which first lived in your grandmother Lois and in your mother Eunice and, I am persuaded, now lives in you also.

2 TIMOTHY 1:5

Before You

We love because he first loved us.

1 JOHN 4:19

There's a popular saying I've seen in pretty wall hangings and vinyl letters for nursery décor lately. It's attributed to Maureen Hawkins and goes like this: "Before you were conceived I wanted you. Before you were born I loved you. Before you were here an hour I would die for you. This is the miracle of life."[4] The statement captures the heart of a mother: that fierce, unconditional love that we feel for our children. Our love for our children precedes sight, precedes existence, and precedes performance. Does that remind you of anyone?

The Scriptures tell us that we love because God first loved us. His love for us preceded creation, it preceded the fall, it preceded our birth, it preceded our failures, it preceded our salvation, it preceded our good works. In short, it preceded everything. From the foundations of the earth, God planned you, He loved you, and He drew you to Himself. In this preceding love we find security, identity, and courage. Human love is inherently risky because we know that we are not guaranteed that our love will be returned. But knowing that we are secure in Christ and loved by Him gives us all we need to risk loving others. It gives us the courage to forgive when wronged, to hope in what we cannot yet see, and to wait patiently in faith. Love has gone before us and given us all we need.

How will the security of God's love enable you to be a better parent? What risks will it allow you to take?

_____

_____

_____

_____

_____

_____

_____

Take a cue from Maureen Hawkins's words and write your own love note to your baby. Tell your dear one about the love you already feel in your heart and what lengths you will go to show that love.

_____

_____

_____

_____

_____

_____

Divine Mission

I have been reminded of your sincere faith,
which first lived in your grandmother
Lois and in your mother Eunice and, I
am persuaded, now lives in you also.

2 TIMOTHY 1:5

*F*rom the scant details we are given about the life of Timothy, we know that he was profoundly shaped by the faith of his mother and grandmother. In 2 Timothy 3:14–15 Paul exhorted Timothy to continue in what he has "learned" and "become convinced of," because he knows those "from whom [he] learned it, and how from infancy [he has] known the holy Scriptures." Eunice's "sincere faith" compelled her to teach Timothy the Scriptures at a tender age (2 Timothy 1:5). The striking maturity that Timothy has as a young man (1 Timothy 4:12) may be rooted in the teaching Timothy had at his mother's knee.

As you prepare to nurture this baby you carry, never for one moment doubt the important ministry God has given you as a mother. You've probably heard the oft-quoted line from poet William Ross Wallace who wrote, "The hand that rocks the cradle is the hand that rules the world." Later in that same poem he implored mothers, "Woman, how divine your mission here upon our natal sod! Keep, oh, keep the young heart open always to the breath of God!"[5] Wallace was reminding young mothers of the kingdom implications of their work. Keep your eye on the big picture. Your sincere faith and your instruction in the way of the Lord will shape this child and, in turn, shape the world.

Motherhood is a high and holy calling, not second-class work. Jesus' chief task in His ministry on earth was molding twelve men into disciples. Likewise, God has called you to one day disciple this child who now grows within you. Write a prayer asking for God's help in carrying out this holy mission and for Him to form you into a woman of sincere faith.

_____

_____

_____

_____

_____

_____

_____

Write a memory of someone—perhaps even your own mother or grandmother—who influenced your faith.

_____

_____

_____

_____

_____

_____

Seek Counsel

Where there is no counsel, the
people fall; but in the multitude
of counselors there is safety.

PROVERBS 11:14 NKJV

You may be procrastinating on finding a crib or stockpiling diapers, but one thing you shouldn't wait on is finding the right pediatrician for your new little bundle. If this is your first baby, you may not even know where to start. That's normal. This is a great opportunity to begin forming some connections with other parents you know and seeking their wisdom. Ask them whom they take their child to and whether they like the doctor's practice. Ask them what was important to them in finding the right pediatrician or what they wish they had kept in mind.

Proverbs offers us good wisdom: Plans fail when there is no guidance. But where there is an abundance of counselors, we find safety. As you move into this journey of parenting, whether this is your first or fourth child, you are going to have plenty of questions. It is not a sign of weakness to ask others for advice; in fact, it's a sign of arrogance not to. Choose your counselors wisely, however. Surround yourself with people whom you respect. And when it comes to important matters of discipline and instruction, make sure you are seeking out wise Christian friends for their input. Loving your child well is too important an endeavor to go it alone. Seek God's wisdom and the counsel of trusted friends and family.

How are you at asking for advice? Do you hate doing it, or is it something you don't mind? In God's economy, needing others is not a bad thing. In fact, it's how He designed us. Make a list of some things related to parenting that you may want to seek advice on.

_____

_____

_____

_____

_____

_____

_____

Have you already gotten good counsel from friends or family about parenting or life with a new baby? If not, who are some people you could begin seeking out?

_____

_____

_____

_____

_____

_____

_____

This Day

This is the day the LORD has made;
let us rejoice and be glad in it.

PSALM 118:24

*T*he balloons are sinking as I write, their helium fading before the party has even begun. My boy turns two today, and the sinking birthday balloons remind me how quickly time passes. It may be a cliché, but truly, it seems only yesterday I cradled this firstborn son, stroked that newborn skin, and was swept away by this tiny one who so radically changed my life. Time is so strange: sometimes it leaves me dizzy with vertigo as the days whoosh past, and other times it leaves me in tears as the minutes drag by. But no matter my perception of it, time's persistent beat reminds me of my call for today: rejoice.

How do we live fully amidst the whoosh and wane of time? We do it by rejoicing in *this* day the Lord has made. We allow ourselves to be glad in *this* day the Lord has given us. We make a conscious choice to be completely present in this present moment, not pining for the past nor living with our heads continually poking into tomorrow.

As you read this, take your hand and place it on your belly. Hold it there and give thanks. Give thanks for this moment of pregnancy. Give thanks for this precious time that is a perfect part of your unfolding story. Sure, there are exciting things ahead (like meeting your little one face-to-face), but today is a gift. This moment is a gift. Be glad and rejoice. This day is grace.

What's going on in your world today? How can you be glad and rejoice in the midst of your circumstances? What does it mean to you to realize this day is a gift—one like none you have ever lived before nor will ever live again?

_____

_____

_____

_____

_____

_____

Dear Little One,

Let me tell you about the love in my heart for you this day . . .

_____

_____

_____

_____

_____

_____

_____

WEEK 31

The Wonder Within

Your womb is getting a bit crowded these days, isn't it? At over 3 pounds and between 15.2 and 16.7 inches long, your little one is looking a lot less wrinkly as fat continues to fill out the body. And because your little tyke is getting so long, around this time he or she will fold in his arms and legs into what is known as the fetal position. While your baby will continue to grow in size and in brain capacity, the lungs are the only system that is not mature enough for unassisted life outside the womb. Eyes, ears, mouth, nose, and skin are fully developed at this point, and the brain is processing sensory information from all five sources.

As you and your little one continue to grow, you may notice your feet swelling. Blood and fluid are being pushed down toward your feet due to the increased pressure of your heavy uterus on the vena cava (the large vein that carries blood from your lower extremities to your heart). There is also a certain amount of water retention that occurs during pregnancy. The best way to counter the swelling is to elevate your feet as much as possible. A bit of swelling in your hands and ankles is normal for the same reasons as well. Getting lots of fluids and staying away from salty foods can also help keep the swelling at bay. However, if you notice excessive swelling in your extremities, as well as puffiness in your face and around your eyes, make sure you call your practitioner. This can be a sign of preeclampsia and should be treated promptly.

Points for Prayer and Praise

- Praise God that all of the major organs except the lungs have likely completed their development. Thank Him for every day your baby gets closer to a healthy full-term delivery.

- Pray for your little one's lungs to complete their development. Pray also that spiritually, your son or daughter may one day learn to give God thanks for every breath that God gives him or her.

- Pray that as your delivery date draws near, you will take your anxious thoughts to Christ and leave your worries at His feet.

Mommy's Memory Verse

The LORD himself goes before you and will be with you; he will never leave you nor forsake you. Do not be afraid; do not be discouraged.

DEUTERONOMY 31:8

Stand by Me

The LORD himself goes before you and will be with you; he will never leave you nor forsake you. Do not be afraid; do not be discouraged.

DEUTERONOMY 31:8

As the big day approaches, I'm sure you are thinking about who you want by your side during labor—your husband, your mom, your sister, a doula—who makes the final cut depends largely on who your go-to people are for comfort and support during physical and emotional stress. Don't feel bad that you must exclude people. Even Jesus took only three of His disciples into closer confidence when He faced His deep trial in the Garden of Gethsemane (Matthew 26:37). It's okay to choose whom you need the most.

But no matter who is with you or who, sadly, can't be, you don't have to face labor and delivery alone. God promises that He will go before His people and that He will never leave nor forsake them. He commands us not to be afraid or discouraged. Why? Because His strength can be our strength, His comforting presence can soothe us, and His mighty arm can defend us. What better labor partner could you have than the omnipotent God?

Will you call on Him in your need or will you rely on yourself? God wants to be your stronghold, your balm, your strength, and your confidence. But He will not force Himself on you. Invite Him today to be the One you turn to in the delivery room.

How does it comfort you to know that God will be beside you
when it comes time for you to deliver? How can you keep this fact
in focus and remember to call upon Him when the time comes?

_____

_____

_____

_____

_____

_____

_____

Whom do you want beside you when it comes time to deliver your
precious baby? Why?

_____

_____

_____

_____

_____

_____

_____

Quiet My Heart

The fruit of righteousness will be
peace; the effect of righteousness will
be quietness and confidence forever.

ISAIAH 32:17

The Bible tells us not to be anxious, but did you know there's an additional reason for you to detoxify your life of anxiety right now? Biologically speaking, a mother's stress increases her blood pressure and heart rate, which in turn increases Baby's heart rate long after Mom's has returned back to normal. Chronic stress in the mother could cause a premature delivery or low birth weight. But it may even have long-term effects. Studies have found that a mother's prolonged anxiety can cause her baby to have a tendency toward stress, making the baby more likely to face chronic health issues like diabetes and heart disease.

As believers, we have a powerful antidote for chronic stress: an almighty God. When we Christians face hardships, we have the comfort of prayer, the confidence of eternal hope, and the peace of God who works all things together for the good of His children. But none of these are much good if we don't take hold of them and claim them for ourselves. When you feel anxious, do you turn those worries into prayers (Philippians 4:6)? When the future grips you with fear, do you remind yourself that you have an eternal, unshakable hope (Isaiah 41:10)? And when the worst happens, do you meditate on the truth that God is working all things together for good (Romans 8:28)? Apply the truths you know and you will see its fruit: peace, quietness, and confidence.

Jesus told us not to worry or be anxious (Matthew 6:25, Philippians 4:6). Do you take these commands seriously? Do you turn your worries into prayers?

_____

_____

_____

_____

_____

_____

Fast-forward into the future: the child you now carry in your womb is about seven or eight years old. One day your child comes home from school, sullen and anxious. That little brow is furrowed, and he or she hardly eats a bite during dinner. What truths from Scripture do you use to help your son or daughter not be anxious?

_____

_____

_____

_____

_____

_____

Enough Love

This is the confidence we have in approaching God: that if we ask anything according to his will, he hears us. And if we know that he hears us—whatever we ask—we know that we have what we asked of him.

1 JOHN 5:14–15

A friend shared that before the birth of their second child, she worried: would she be able to love a new child with the same fierce love that she had for her first? While I never personally wrestled with this fear, I have had a few of my own. How would my son adjust to his new sibling? How would I adjust to the expanding duties of motherhood? No matter how many children we've had, all of us have fears when it comes to change. And many of those fears revolve around one question: "Will I have what it takes?"

But here's a better question: "Do I truly depend on God?" God doesn't promise us that we will love or parent perfectly. In fact, our failures may even be what lead our children to know that only God can fully satisfy. But as we look to God in dependence, He loves to answer the prayers of His children. He longs for you to love well, to walk before your children in faith and righteousness, to discipline and instruct them in His ways. So whatever your worries, don't wallow in them; take them to Christ. He will give you exactly what you need to love this little one well.

Have you ever thought about the fact that your shortcomings may be a part of God's plan for your children to know their need of Him? What would happen if we could fully satisfy our children's every need or wish?

_____

_____

_____

_____

_____

_____

_____

_____

What adjustments will this new baby mean for you and your family? Take some time to pray about these changes and ask God for His help as you or other members of your family face them.

_____

_____

_____

_____

_____

_____

_____

Resting in Him

The God who made the world and everything
in it is the Lord of heaven and earth and
does not live in temples built by hands. And
he is not served by human hands, as if he
needed anything, because he himself gives all
men life and breath and everything else.

ACTS 17:24–25

Perhaps you've heard these two difficult words from your doctor: *bed rest.* Or perhaps you've found you can't do all the things you could before. The end of pregnancy often finds us in the position of having to ask for help. If you are a do-it-all kind of woman, this can be a bitter pill.

When I was younger, I read the biography of Amy Carmichael, a famous missionary to India who cared for orphaned children. The thing that made the biggest impression on me was what she learned at the end of her life. After a lifetime of doing for Jesus, she was stuck in bed. While her mind was strong, her body was not. And for the first time, she learned that God did not love her for what she did for Him— as if God needs anything from us—but that He loved her. He simply loved her.[6]

While God certainly is pleased when we join Him in serving others, He does not need us. He loves us even when all we can do is lie in bed. He loves us for who we are in Him.

Do you struggle with the need to constantly be doing? Your worth is not found in your constant motion; it is found in Christ, just as you are. He already did what was needed. Reflect on the finished work of Christ. What does it mean to know God doesn't love you for what you do for Him?

_____

_____

_____

_____

_____

_____

_____

Similarly, God wants us to love Him not for His gifts but for who He is. If many of His good gifts were taken from you, would you still love Him? Tell God today you love Him, not just His good gifts.

_____

_____

_____

_____

_____

_____

WEEK 32

The Wonder Within

It's just six to ten weeks before showtime, and your little one is practicing hard for opening day. Sucking, practice breathing, blinking, touching, moving the amniotic fluid into the mouth and down into the digestive system—namely, all the skills your baby will need for the first months of life outside the womb. Baby is weighing in at about 3.75 pounds and measuring between 15.2 and 16.7 inches long. You may notice your little one's movements decreasing as room in the womb is growing scarce. And in the next few weeks, he or she will likely settle in the head-down position in preparation for birth.

Meanwhile, you're gaining about a pound a week and roughly half of that goes directly to your baby. You'll likely begin seeing your practitioner twice a month now. If you feel your stomach tightening up and growing hard, you may be experiencing what are called Braxton Hicks contractions. While these are false contractions, it is important to pay attention to them. If they grow in intensity and come at regular or shorter intervals (particularly if you have more than four episodes in an hour), you may be experiencing preterm labor. If so, call your practitioner at once. Otherwise, try not to worry about them and give thanks that God is already preparing your body for labor.

POINTS FOR PRAYER AND PRAISE

- Praise God for how your baby continues to gain weight, insulating him or her for life after birth.
- Pray for your little one as he or she practices all the skills that will be needed for the first months of life outside the womb. Pray also that as your little one grows, your son or daughter would put his or her faith into practice.
- Pray for yourself that God would give you discernment to know when and if you need to call your doctor or midwife before Baby is due—and that you will be prepared should labor come early.

MOMMY'S MEMORY VERSE

Six days you shall labor and do all your work, but the seventh day is a Sabbath to the LORD your God.

EXODUS 20:9–10

Center of Gravity

In Him we live and move and have our
being, as also some of your own poets have
said, "For we are also His offspring."

ACTS 17:28 NKJV

I remember coming down the stairs one day during my first pregnancy and slipping. Kaboom-boom-boom. Thankfully, I landed firmly on my bottom, and aside from a dark blue bruise, the fall did no harm to me or to the baby. If you're feeling a little clumsier than usual, there's good reason. As your belly grows, your center of gravity shifts. It can throw your balance quite off. Couple that with the increased dizziness that comes with pregnancy (due to your growing uterus putting pressure on blood vessels), and you've got a recipe for one clumsy mama.

In our spiritual lives too, sometimes small changes can throw off our sense of balance. A business trip disrupts our daily quiet time routine or a sick baby keeps us home from church several weeks in a row. Before we know it, we find ourselves off-kilter spiritually, snapping or being critical when we should be showing grace, or falling into covetousness instead of choosing contentment. When we find ourselves like this, we must run back to Christ. He is our center. Our life is balanced when we abide in Him. In Him "we live and move and have our being." Everything depends on Him. And no priority in our lives will be in its right place unless He has the first and supreme position. He is the still point of our turning world. Stay close to Him and everything else will fall into its proper place.

God has given us the means of grace (prayer, quiet time, fellowship, hearing His Word, memorizing Scripture, fasting, etc.) to keep us in balance spiritually. But it takes self-discipline to sustain these practices in the first place. The good news: God also gives us self-discipline (2 Timothy 1:7). Write a prayer asking for God's help to sustain your spiritual disciplines both now and in the months ahead.

_____

_____

_____

_____

_____

Meditating on Scripture is one of the things that keeps us balanced. Write to your little one about one of your favorite Bible verses to meditate upon and why that verse is so meaningful to you.

_____

_____

_____

_____

_____

_____

The Wonder of You

*We have different gifts, according
to the grace given us.*

ROMANS 12:6

*H*ave you found yourself wondering lately what your precious baby will be like? Will she have Daddy's curly hair or your silly sense of humor? Will he be daring or more reserved and thoughtful? Will your mother's gifts in art skip a generation? Only time will tell. But this much is certain: your son or daughter will be utterly unique, a masterpiece created by the living God and endowed with his or her own particular gifts for this particular time.

The uniqueness of your child is certainly reason to pause and praise God. Never before nor never again will this exact personality exist. And as a creature made in the image of God, he or she will offer a particular insight into God's own character. While you will certainly see shades of yourself and your husband in this little life, you must always remember that you are dealing with an absolutely unique personality.

As you stop to marvel at the incredible miracle of this unique being whom you will soon meet, let the wonder lead you to worship. Think about the incredible diversity of the human race. Each person over the entire span of human history has been made completely unique. What does this tell us about the vastness and creativity of God? Worship this God who has made you and this child you carry so "fearfully and wonderfully" (Psalm 139:14).

What does the uniqueness of each human creation tell you about the Creator?

_____

_____

_____

_____

_____

_____

_____

What traits do you think you inherited from your mom? from your dad? In what ways are you strikingly different from them? Tell your little one about it here.

_____

_____

_____

_____

_____

_____

_____

Real or Not?

*Anyone who runs ahead and does not
continue in the teaching of Christ does
not have God; whoever continues in the
teaching has both the Father and the Son.*

2 JOHN 1:9

As I write this, I'm bleary-eyed from staying up late counting the minutes between episodes of my stomach tightening up like a drum. After an hour of contractions coming between ten to fifteen minutes apart, I called my midwife. "How can I tell if this is preterm labor or just Braxton Hicks?" I asked. "The only way you know for sure," she said, "is whether the experience continues and grows in intensity." Labor that is real is labor that continues. Thankfully, in my case, with a warm bath and a good night's sleep, it disappeared.

When it comes to our spiritual lives, we know that faith that is truly real is faith that continues to grow and bear fruit in our lives. While we are not saved by our works, our works show the reality of our salvation. And the proof that we are true followers of Christ is found in whether we continue in the faith. So how about you? When you look at your life, do you see branches hanging heavy with fruit, or do you see a parched and dead patch of land? That's not to say that true believers won't walk through dry spells. But faith that is real is faith that ultimately continues. It is a faith that perseveres.

In Matthew 7:21–22 we see that though we may look like Christians on the outside, what really matters is the condition of our heart. In what ways do you see evidence in your life that you are seeking to do the will of the Father and continuing in the faith?

_____

_____

_____

_____

_____

_____

Have you thought through what your action plan would be if you go into labor early? Whom will you call on to give you a ride if your husband can't get there quickly enough? Who can get there quickly to care for your other children?

_____

_____

_____

_____

_____

_____

A Rhythm of Rest

*Six days you shall labor and do all
your work, but the seventh day is a
Sabbath to the LORD your God.*

EXODUS 20:9–10

*D*oes your pre-baby "to do" list have you exhausted? Whenever I find myself worn-out and lacking margin, the first question I ask is whether I've been leaning into God's rhythm of rest. The Sabbath is really important to God—so much that He put it in His Ten Commandments (the most important top-ten list of all time!). And by ordering our lives around it, we find true rest—rest for mind, body, and soul.

Once you have children, the Sabbath changes. You can't skip diaper changes or night feedings. But even in the midst of the responsibilities of caring for children, you can find ways to take resting seriously on the Sabbath day. Try, for example, to plan simple meals. Use that crockpot or, better yet, make a casserole the night before. Save your chores—laundry, housecleaning, grocery shopping—for other days. If your "to do" list usually overrides napping, commit to putting the list aside at least on the Sabbath and taking that nap or spending some quality time alone with God. Make the Sabbath a special time of connecting with your spouse, with a good friend, or with a new family visiting your church. If you lean into God's grace, He will bless you with enough time to accomplish His will for you each day. And in the process you will find your heart, body, and soul rejuvenated.

Do you take God's command to order your life around the Sabbath seriously? How could you improve, keeping in mind that God has made this day not as a burden but as a source of relief and healing for His people?

_____

_____

_____

_____

_____

_____

The Sabbath can be a really special day for your family. What kinds of habits or traditions will you make part of your family's observance of the Sabbath? Attending church together, having others over for a nice meal, playing games together, going for a walk, or reading God's Word together are just a few ideas.

_____

_____

_____

_____

_____

WEEK 33

The Wonder Within

*H*ave you seen a knee or tiny foot make a visible ripple across your belly yet? It's amazing, isn't it? Well, if such sights and sensations haven't clued you in yet, your baby is running out of real estate. In fact, as your little one gains weight and grows in size, there is less amniotic fluid surrounding him. That means less cushioning inside and, in turn, you feel those kicks and stretches more than ever. And speaking of gaining, your baby may already be over 4 pounds this week and stretching between 17.2 and 18.7 inches long (about the length of a bunch of leeks). One aspect of God's marvelous design of your little one is the fact that Baby's bones still haven't fused together totally. This makes it possible for the bones, particularly in the head, to move and slightly overlap for an easier time fitting through the birth canal. And it's also the reason your little wonder may temporarily sport a cone-head in those early baby pictures.

Make sure you are continuing to do your daily kick or fetal movement counts during baby's active periods. (Talk to your own health-care provider for specifics.) But as a general rule of thumb, your baby should have at least one active period a day in which you are able to note ten fetal movements within about an hour. If you haven't noticed an active period within the course of a day, lie down on your side or drink some juice and see if you don't feel a nudge soon. Call your practitioner if movement has significantly lessened or if you are not having an active period of at least ten movements in about an hour. Your practitioner can always have you come in and monitor the baby just for some extra peace of mind.

POINTS FOR PRAYER AND PRAISE

- If you've been able to experience the wonder of seeing your baby's contours ripple across your belly, praise God for this. Life is a gift and a miracle.
- Pray for your baby as his or her memory begins strengthening in the womb. Pray also that as your son or daughter grows, God will bless him or her with many sweet memories and heal any bitter ones.
- Pray for yourself as you prepare for labor, that you will be as ready as possible spiritually, physically, intellectually, and emotionally.

MOMMY'S MEMORY VERSE

Jesus grew in wisdom and stature, and in favor with God and men.

LUKE 2:52

Not Your Own

You are not your own; you were bought at a
price. Therefore honor God with your body.

1 CORINTHIANS 6:19–20

There comes a point in every pregnancy when you are just ready to have your body back: to fit in your skinny jeans again and drink venti lattes to your heart's content. Pregnancy, and motherhood in general, stretches us to the limits of sacrifice. Even after that little one comes, our bodies are not our own. If you're breast-feeding, you'll still be thinking about whether the coffee you consume is what's keeping Junior from napping. Or maybe you're ready for a night out, but can't leave your little one with a sitter quite yet. Every mother can empathize.

But here's something to consider. The Bible tells us that none of us is "our own." We belong to Jesus. We are, therefore, to honor Him with our bodies. When in our flesh we just can't give any more, we pray, "Oh God, help me." Perhaps He wants you to continue giving in an area in which you're feeling drained. If this is the case, if you call to Him in faith, He will give you the strength you need. Or perhaps He knows you sincerely need a time to recharge in order to serve those in your care. If you look to Him in faith, He will make a way. He will give you what you need. After all, you are not your own; you are His. And He cares for His precious ones.

When you are at the end of your strength, do you just gut your way through it, or do you pray? Are there any typical points in the day when you tend to feel like you have nothing left to give? Maybe when driving home from work or when putting your other children to bed? Try placing some reminders at strategic places to remind you to stop and pray.

_____

_____

_____

_____

_____

_____

In all likelihood you have between six and ten weeks left of pregnancy. Write a prayer for your baby as his or her development in the womb continues and pray that you will also have the endurance and peace you need for the last leg of the journey.

_____

_____

_____

_____

_____

_____

Memory Awakens

*"I will forgive their wickedness and
will remember their sins no more."*

HEBREWS 8:12

*R*ecent studies indicate that even as early as thirty weeks, babies in the womb are beginning to form short-term memory.[7] Babies both in utero and outside the womb show a higher level of interest in something new than to stimuli to which they have been previously exposed (habituation). By studying the measure of habituation, scientists have been able to determine that by thirty weeks, a fetus is developing the ability to remember sounds that he has been exposed to before. Talk about a good impetus for reading, singing, and talking to your little one now!

The human memory is a dazzling thing. Our ability to store and retrieve previous sights, sounds, and smells is phenomenal and unparalleled in the world of living creatures. But because of the fall, our memories are often full of painful events or sinful images we wish were not there. Yet the omniscient God who has seen the atrocities of all generations chooses to "remember no more" the sins of those who turn to Him in faith. "As far as the east is from the west," He wipes our transgressions from us (Psalm 103:12). And He commands us not to keep a "record of wrongs" for those who have transgressed against us (1 Corinthians 13:5), but instead forgive as we have been forgiven (Ephesians 4:32). God wants to be Lord and Healer even over our memories.

All of us have memories they wish were not there. Have you ever thought about taking your painful memories to God and asking Him for healing? Consider doing so now.

_____

_____

_____

_____

_____

_____

_____

_____

Write a prayer for your little one that the things of God will be part of even his or her earliest memories.

_____

_____

_____

_____

_____

_____

_____

Grow, Baby, Grow!

Jesus grew in wisdom and stature,
and in favor with God and men.

LUKE 2:52

*W*hile you may feel like there's no room for your belly to expand another inch, no one sent that memo to your little one. He or she is packing on almost a half pound every week. And lengthwise, you can expect him or her to grow almost a full inch this week!

As you think about your little one growing, pray for future growth as well. The Bible tells us relatively little about the childhood of Jesus, save for one story about Him in the temple and this verse: "Jesus grew in wisdom and stature, and in favor with God and men" (Luke 2:52). But what we do know from this verse is that Christ grew in a holistic fashion. God wasn't just concerned about Jesus' physical growth, but His intellectual, social, and spiritual growth as well. He was growing wise—a word that refers not simply to knowledge but to the fear of the Lord (Proverbs 9:10). Jesus was growing in favor with God and with man, keeping the Great Commandment to love the Lord His God with all that He had and to love His neighbor as Himself (Matthew 22:36–40). So, as you see the number on your scale inching up this week, rejoice in your little one's growth, and pray for his or her future growth to mirror the holistic pattern of Christ.

As you look at your life, do you see the kind of balance evident in Christ's childhood? Do you care for your physical body at the expense of your spiritual life, or do you focus on the intellectual to the exclusion of the social?

_____

_____

_____

_____

_____

_____

Write a prayer for your baby's physical growth today as well as for his or her holistic growth (wisdom, stature, favor with God and man) in the future.

_____

_____

_____

_____

_____

_____

_____

_____

Date Night

His mouth is most sweet, yes, he is
altogether lovely. This is my beloved, and
this is my friend, O daughters of Jerusalem!
SONG OF SONGS 5:16 NKJV

The big day is right around the corner, and if you haven't gotten away with your husband for a date night (or a weekend!), get it on the calendar, pronto! Do whatever you've got to do to make it happen: find a sitter for your older kids, cut coupons for a favorite restaurant, or ask the boss for a Saturday off. Just make time with your sweetie a priority. For us, Valentine's Day fell a few weeks before my first son was born. So my husband and I decided to "get away" a few blocks from the hospital where I was to deliver. We chuckled that we would be closer to the hospital if I went into labor.

While it's easier to make time with your spouse a priority before the baby, don't let this habit fall by the wayside once Baby comes. And when you make that time, do what the Song of Songs models for us: praise your husband. Remind him of all the reasons you married him and why you are so deeply attracted to him. Cultivate the romance, remembering that he is your beloved, and cultivate sharing and companionship, remembering that he is also your friend. You will always be a parent, but do not forget that you are first and foremost a lover and a friend to your spouse.

What character qualities do you admire most about your husband?

_____

_____

_____

_____

_____

_____

_____

_____

Make an action plan. When can you get a date night on the calendar? What are some ideas for what you can do? What logistics do you need to work out to make it happen?

_____

_____

_____

_____

_____

_____

WEEK 34

The Wonder Within

*Y*our little wonder continues filling out this week, weighing in at around 4.7 pounds and stretching between 17.2 and 18.7 inches long. (No wonder you're feeling so big, huh?) Baby is also accumulating your antibodies, which you can continue passing on to your infant after birth through breast milk. That's one of many reasons why the American Academy of Pediatrics encourages mothers to breast-feed exclusively for the first six months. Aside from gaining antibodies and weight, your little one may be moving into prime position for birth. Around this point many babies move from their curled up position at the top of the uterus into head-down position, with the head resting on your pubic bone. When people tell you that it looks like the baby has dropped, this is what they mean.

When Baby does drop, that equals both good news and bad news for you, Mama. First, the bad news: the increased pressure below may occasionally pinch your sciatic nerve, giving you shooting pain up the back. It may also cause you to waddle a bit more when you walk. The good news, however, is that breathing and heartburn might get better. And here's some more good news: babies born between thirty-four and thirty-seven weeks with no other health issues generally do fine after a short stay in the NICU. That's not to say you want your baby to come earlier than full-term (let him or her take as long as needed), but let this fact ease your mind. You and your little one have both come a long way since the beginning of this pregnancy journey.

Points for Prayer and Praise

🪇 Praise God that, after a short stay in NICU, most babies born between thirty-four and thirty-seven weeks and who show no other signs of health issues generally do as well as their full-term peers.

🪇 Pray for your little one as his or her immune system continues preparing its defenses. Pray also that as your son or daughter matures in the Christian faith, he or she will be strong to ward off attacks from the world, the flesh, and the evil one.

🪇 Pray that you will continue to press on to know Christ and to make Him known as you continue the journey ahead. Pray that you will see motherhood's call as a noble ambition.

Mommy's Memory Verse

All Scripture is God-breathed and is useful for teaching, rebuking, correcting and training in righteousness.

2 Timothy 3:16

Lofty Ambitions

*I want to know Christ and the power
of his resurrection and the fellowship of
sharing in his sufferings, becoming like
him in his death, and so, somehow, to
attain to the resurrection from the dead.*

PHILIPPIANS 3:10–11

In a little more than a month, life will change forever for you. You will welcome a new child, embracing both this little one and the calling God has given you. Whether this is your first child or not, each transition is a challenge. And with each new life under your care, this thing we used to know called "free time" dwindles. Perhaps you'll be transitioning from a fast-paced career or from a life with more independent children. Whatever the case, it can seem like lofty ambitions are now a thing of the past. Right now your ambition is to get a hot shower each day!

But while you may think weighty ambitions belong to a life you are leaving behind, they certainly do not. Paul shared his goal with the church of Phillipi, saying, "I want to know Christ." There is no greater aspiration than this. And despite your changing circumstances, you can still press on to take hold of Him. In fact, as you die to yourself daily as a mother, you will know more of Christ, who fully poured out Himself on our behalf. As you press on "to know Christ," your holy calling also expands to help your little one know Him. To know Him and to make Him known—there's no greater ambition than this.

As moms of little ones, we can easily feel tied down. Isn't it nice to remember Paul wrote these words from a prison cell? No matter our constraints, God wants us to pursue the lofty goal of knowing Him more. How do you think this new season of your life may actually help you know Christ better?

_____

_____

_____

_____

_____

_____

Ambition is a good thing when it is driven by a passion for Christ. You don't even have to have a religious goal for God to be pleased. He wants us to do everything we do for His glory. Write a prayer asking God to give your children holy ambitions—ones that are pure in their motive to glorify Him.

_____

_____

_____

_____

_____

_____

Altogether Lovely

All beautiful you are, my darling;
there is no flaw in you.

SONG OF SONGS 4:7

*I*f you are anything like me, at thirty-four weeks you are feeling as big as a house. And there are still weeks (and pounds!) to go until D-Day—delivery day, that is. Even those maternity clothes that seemed as though they could house Jolly Old Saint Nick only a few months ago are now starting to feel snug. Exhaustion has effaced whatever pregnancy glow you might have felt a few months ago. And when you look in the mirror, you have to squint to see your old self.

If you are feeling far from lovely these days, remember how God sees you. While the book of Song of Songs is certainly about marital love, it is also about the love of God and His church. And when God looks at us, robed as we are in the righteousness of Christ, He sees perfection. He sees no flaw, only deep and true beauty.

What's more, while notions in our culture may conspire to make us feel unlovely during pregnancy, God created us and our bodies to do this very thing: to nurture and house a little life. Will you tell the Maker that His design is faulty and ugly? Or will you look with His eyes to see the beauty of what He's created? Believe the words He speaks over you: "All beautiful you are, my darling; there is no flaw in you."

Benjamin Franklin once said there were two things that took his breath away: a ship in full sails and the beauty of a pregnant woman, round and full with life.[8] What cultural notions inform your view of your pregnant body? Do those notions agree with God's view of you?

_____

_____

_____

_____

_____

_____

_____

Every boy or girl who comes into this world will struggle at some point with body image. Too tall, too short, too skinny, too plump— all of us struggle with something. Write a prayer for your son or daughter that he or she will be secure and confident, resting in God's approval and not this world's.

_____

_____

_____

_____

_____

_____

_____

Hide It Away

All Scripture is God-breathed and is useful for teaching, rebuking, correcting and training in righteousness.

2 TIMOTHY 3:16

*I*f the days toward your due date are dragging, remember there's plenty to do. You're probably already tucking away piles of diapers in the nursery, storing casseroles in the freezer, and stowing receiving blankets in the closet. But while you're preparing for the future, take time to hide away some Scripture in your heart for the days ahead. While it may not be at the top of the nesting "to do" list, it will certainly prove helpful.

Paul told Timothy, "*All* Scripture is God-breathed and is useful for teaching, rebuking, correcting and training in righteousness" (2 Timothy 3:16, italics mine). Hmm . . . do any of those activities sound like things you might be doing for the next eighteen years? You bet.

Having God's Word hidden in your heart will be good not only for you but also for your little one. It will help you raise your children not only to act rightly but also to be remade into the likeness of Christ. Using Scripture in your correction and training will lend power to your efforts. Isaiah 55:11 says, "So is my word that goes out from my mouth: it will not return to me empty, but will accomplish what I desire." What a comfort to know that as we use God's words in training our children, our attempts won't return empty! How many other parenting tips have that kind of return on their investment?

In what areas of training your children will it be helpful for you to know Scripture? Do any verses come to mind that you would like to commit to memory?

_____

_____

_____

_____

_____

_____

_____

Do you have a life verse you often turn to? Tell your little one about it.

_____

_____

_____

_____

_____

_____

_____

God's Tattoo Parlor

[Jesus] said to Thomas, "Put your finger here; see my hands. Reach out your hand and put it into my side."

JOHN 20:27

It's only natural to wonder if your body will ever be the same after childbirth. Whether because of unsightly stretch marks or because of feet that have morphed into the monstrous shoe size of Cinderella's ugly stepsister, most women experience some anxiety about their body's changes. In some cases the changes are temporary; in others they are permanent.

Singer and songwriter Jennifer Daniels shares the story of how she nearly lost her twin babies when she went into premature labor. To save their lives, the doctor ordered an emergency C-section. In her song "Tattoo" Daniels imagines one day her son and daughter asking about her scar: "Mama, tell that one again, the one about the scar that stretches out across your skin so far. Don't leave out the part where you call it the tattoo that God in all His love picked out for you." She concludes the song with the line, "If Jesus wears His scars for me, then I'll wear mine for you."[9]

God could have removed Christ's scars when He raised Him from the dead. Instead, He left them as a sign of His great love for us. Whether your body completely bounces back or not, you can choose how you wear the marks of motherhood. Will you feel sorry for yourself or see your scars as a testimony of your love?

Think for a moment about the scars of Jesus and the way they shout His love for you. How does meditating on this change your view of your body's changes? What words do you think Christ would use to describe your value to Him?

_____

_____

_____

_____

_____

_____

_____

Scars, whether physical or emotional, point back to the things we have endured and point forward to Christ's amazing power of healing. What healing have you experienced from God's hand?

_____

_____

_____

_____

_____

_____

_____

WEEK 35

The Wonder Within

*T*his week your little wonder is 5.25 pounds and stretching between 17.2 and 18.7 inches long. Your little pumpkin's brain development continues to be a key component in these last weeks of uterine stay. In fact, researchers believe both learning and memory are already occurring in the womb. For instance, newborns seem to show preference not only for their own mother's voice but also for books and lullabies they have heard in utero. Research has found similar preferences for tastes that your baby is exposed to in the womb, particularly those in the final weeks of pregnancy when memory seems to sharpen.

While your baby is learning to remember your voice, you are hoping to remember everything you need to pack for your hospital bag! While there's still time before your due date, it doesn't hurt to pack that bag now, have phone numbers for your health-care providers, and a plan for getting to the hospital and, if this isn't your first baby, arranging child care. Consider touring your hospital or birthing center now so you're better oriented once labor has begun. Do you know where to go once you get inside? Can you preregister now so that you'll have less paperwork later? Knowing this kind of information will help make delivery day go as smoothly as possible.

Points for Prayer and Praise

- Praise God for the way He continues to develop your little one's mind in the womb in these final weeks of pregnancy.
- Pray for your baby's developing sleep patterns, both now and after arrival. Pray also that as your son or daughter grows into adulthood, he or she will learn to rest in the Lord.
- Pray for your own attitude during these final weeks of pregnancy. Pray that despite physical discomfort, you will still exhibit joy and gratitude for the blessing of this child. Pray also that you will not be anxious, but cast your cares at the feet of Jesus.

Mommy's Memory Verse

We are hard pressed on every side, but not crushed; perplexed, but not in despair; persecuted, but not abandoned; struck down, but not destroyed.

2 Corinthians 4:8–9

Nesting

*"As long as it is day, we must do the
work of him who sent me. Night is
coming, when no one can work."*

JOHN 9:4

*H*as it begun yet? Have you found yourself cleaning cabinets, scrubbing floors, freezing meals, and organizing closets? Despite how exhausted you are, you can't seem to sit still. If so, you've definitely hit the nesting phase at full throttle. And once that baby arrives, you'll be grateful, because cleaning, cooking, and organizing will be the last things on your mind. After all, who wants to do chores when you've got a precious newborn to nuzzle and rock?

The funny thing about nesting is the urgency with which it hits us. At some point in the third trimester, we realize time is running out and we best be getting busy. Jesus wants us to have that same kind of urgency when it comes to doing work for the kingdom. He said, "As long as it is day, we must do the work of him who sent me. Night is coming, when no one can work" (John 9:4).

With each day that passes, His return is getting closer. Friends and family need to hear the message of the gospel before they face their own life's end or before He comes again. The inevitability of "night" is certain. Our time for doing His work and sharing the good news is limited. Let's roll up our sleeves and get to work!

Time on this earth is finite for all of us. No one is guaranteed a tomorrow. And none of us know when Christ might return. Does this urgency penetrate your heart? More importantly, does it spur you to do anything differently?

_____

_____

_____

_____

_____

_____

_____

What are some of the things on your nesting "to do" list? If you've already found yourself nesting, tell your little one about it.

_____

_____

_____

_____

_____

_____

Returning Thanks

*One of [the ten lepers], when he saw he was
healed, came back, praising God in a loud
voice. He threw himself at Jesus' feet and
thanked him—and he was a Samaritan.*

LUKE 17:15–16

*B*aby gifts from friends and family are such a blessing. But are you knee-deep in writing thank-you notes now? Thankfully, the baby belly makes a nice little lap desk for writing to those who have been so generous.

It's important to stop and give thanks for the ways others have been kind to us. But too many times we fail to give thanks to the most important Giver of all. Like the other nine lepers who were healed, we quickly run off and forget to thank Jesus at all.

Above my son's crib, my husband and I put the words of 1 Samuel 1:27: "I prayed for this child, and the LORD has granted me what I asked of him." That verse has often encouraged me to stop and thank God for the blessing of my son. In those new days of joy, on the nights when I rocked and rocked him because he wouldn't stop crying, amidst the first coos on the changing table and the tantrums that came later on, again and again I remembered, "For *this* child I have prayed, and God has granted my desire." Thanking God for *this* child has kept each day with him in the right perspective.

Write a prayer of thanksgiving to God for the precious gift of your child.

_____

_____

_____

_____

_____

_____

_____

_____

What special gifts or acts of kindness on behalf of your new little one have made you particularly grateful?

_____

_____

_____

_____

_____

_____

_____

Date:

_____

Preparing for Labor

We are hard pressed on every side,
but not crushed; perplexed, but not in
despair; persecuted, but not abandoned;
struck down, but not destroyed.

2 CORINTHIANS 4:8–9

*A*s you near the end of pregnancy, it's natural to be preoccupied with labor. Will your water break at home or at church? Will you labor for days or barely have time to get to the hospital?

Well if there is anything you can count on, it is this: labor is called labor because it's hard work. The Bible does not sugarcoat a process that, while natural and made by God, has been tainted by the fall. Labor is not easy.

But here's an equally important truth: God will be with you every moment, never leaving your side. And whether your struggle has been great or small, in the end it will grow dim in the light of your joy as you smell baby-soft skin, feel tiny clutching fingers, and gaze into those steely newborn eyes.

Prepare for the labor ahead by practicing trusting God. While trusting God is a mental and spiritual act, it has very tangible ramifications. When we relax in God's truths, our heart grows lighter, our fists unclench, our shoulders relax, and our breathing slows. Rehearse today the things you know of God: He is good. He loves you. He is here for you. He will never leave you nor forsake you. Practice resting in these truths, dear one, and do not be afraid.

List some verses that bring you comfort in difficult times. Pack this list in your hospital bag and consider asking your husband or someone in the labor room to read the verses aloud when you get anxious.

_____

_____

_____

_____

_____

_____

_____

Dear Little One,

To get ready for your big entrance into the world, your father and I [list books you read, classes you took, or any other preparations you made] . . .

_____

_____

_____

_____

_____

_____

_____

Grouchy or Grateful?

The rabble with them began to crave other
food, and again the Israelites started wailing
and said, "If only we had meat to eat! We
remember the fish we ate in Egypt at no cost—
also the cucumbers, melons, leeks, onions and
garlic. But now we have lost our appetite;
we never see anything but this manna!"

NUMBERS 11:4–6

*A*h, the third trimester! There's so much to grumble about: back-aches, midnight leg spasms, constant trips to the bathroom, the impending pain of labor, the steady up-up-and-away of the scale. Amidst it all, we can easily lose perspective. Most likely, this is a baby for whom you prayed earnestly. Next, these afflictions have an end in sight . . . somewhere within a couple weeks of your due date. And finally, for every woman who complains about such discomforts, another woman endured them on her behalf.

Often we forget—or fool ourselves—about complaining. We treat it like it's not a sin, when in fact, if you look at the story of the Israelites wandering in the wilderness for forty years, you will see it was because of their ingratitude. They couldn't keep the mercies of God in sight for one minute: He'd brought them out of Egypt (with booty no less!), He'd provided them with food, and He was personally leading them to the promised land. These complainers were framed all around by the mercies of God; we are more like them than we sometimes care to admit.

Where do you see the grace of God in your past, in your present, and in your future? Does meditating on these things make you want to grumble less?

_____

_____

_____

_____

_____

_____

_____

What are some ways you hope to cultivate a grateful heart in your child?

_____

_____

_____

_____

_____

_____

_____

_____

WEEK 36

The Wonder Within

At around 5.7 pounds and stretching between 17.2 and 18.7 inches long, your little one is about 15 percent body fat. That's great news for new life outside the womb when Baby's brain and body fat will be key for maintaining a healthy body temperature. Other developments inside the womb this week include increasing muscle tone (in fact, you may be surprised at just how strong your baby's gripping reflex is), shedding of the lanugo and the vernix caseosa (though you will likely still see a bit at birth), and continuing development of surfactant in the lungs (which will be necessary for strong lung function when Baby draws that first breath).

How about you? Are you waddling yet? If Baby has dropped, you've probably adopted that infamous late-pregnancy shuffle. The loosening of your muscles due to the hormone relaxin, along with the baby's low position, are making even the walk from the parking lot into the grocery store challenging. As the weeks draw near for Baby's arrival, take time out and put your feet up. Rest as much as you can so that your body can be physically recharged should labor come unexpectedly. While you're at it, you can recharge your spiritual batteries too. There will be nothing more comforting come delivery day than feeling God's close presence with you in the delivery room.

Points for Prayer and Praise

- Praise God for all the final work that is happening in the womb as Baby gets ready for prime time. Praise Him for how your body is getting ready for the big day too.
- Pray for your baby's muscle tone development. Pray also that as he or she grows, your son or daughter would exercise the spiritual muscles of self-control and self-discipline.
- Pray for yourself, that you are ready when delivery day comes—with your bags packed, necessary arrangements in order, and your mind at peace, fully trusting in Him.

Mommy's Memory Verse

I will greatly rejoice in the LORD, my soul shall be joyful in my God; for He has clothed me with the garments of salvation, He has covered me with the robe of righteousness.

ISAIAH 61:10 NKJV

Be Ready

You know very well that the day of the Lord will come like a thief in the night. While people are saying, "Peace and safety," destruction will come on them suddenly, as labor pains on a pregnant woman, and they will not escape.

1 THESSALONIANS 5:2–3

$\mathcal{B}$aby clothes washed, car seat installed, hospital bag packed: I just crossed the last major item off my baby "to do" list today and am breathing a huge sigh of relief. While the baby most likely won't come for another several weeks, there's always a possibility he may arrive early.

When Paul addressed the church of Thessalonica, he used labor as a metaphor for the Lord's return. That day, he said, would be unexpected. It would come suddenly like a thief in the night. And like labor, there would be no escaping it once the day of the Lord came. Why was Paul saying this? Was he trying to scare the Thessalonians? No, in fact, he was encouraging them as they faced persecution by saying Christ could return at any time; His return would be the best news they could receive, after all. How should they be prepared? They should "be self-controlled, putting on faith and love as a breastplate, and the hope of salvation as a helmet" (1 Thessalonians 5:8). In other words, they should guard their minds with the assurance of their salvation while they actively exercise faith and love toward others. Although the day of Christ's coming will be a surprise, His people should be ready.

When you think about the day of the Lord's Second Coming, do you feel prepared? How would your everyday actions and attitudes change if you truly lived out the truth that His return could happen at any time?

_____

_____

_____

_____

_____

_____

_____

What's left on your "to do" list before Baby's arrival? Don't stress. Pray for God's grace to help you with the tasks you still need to accomplish and ask Him for the peace not to worry about things that may not get done.

_____

_____

_____

_____

_____

_____

_____

Date:

- - - - - - - - - -

Coming-Home Outfit

I will greatly rejoice in the LORD, my soul
shall be joyful in my God; for He has clothed
me with the garments of salvation, He has
covered me with the robe of righteousness.

ISAIAH 61:10 NKJV

I'd picked out two outfits with all the care and love a first-time mother could have in her heart. One was pink with ruffles on the bottom and one was blue with choo-choo train overalls, and as a reflection of my first-time status, both were about three times too big for the little bundle I brought home from the hospital.

Picking out a coming-home outfit for your little one can be such a joy. Who knew that tiny socks and shoes could flood you with so much happiness? Well, God has also picked out a coming-home outfit for you, and it shouldn't surprise you that it is splendid. The book of Isaiah tells us that we are "clothed . . . with garments of salvation" and "arrayed . . . in a robe of righteousness." When we come face-to-face with God, we will stand not in our own paltry rags—the good deeds we have done—but in the perfect, righteous covering of Christ. This is also the reason we can boldly approach God in prayer. We come not by our own merit, but by the merit of Christ. God sees us not covered in the dirt and grime of our past sins and failures, but in the perfect, spotless righteousness of His Son. That's some coming-home outfit!

The very first sacrifice recorded in the Bible occurred after the fall. God Himself killed an animal and from its skins sewed a covering for Adam's and Eve's nakedness (Genesis 3:21). That sacrifice prefigures Christ's atoning death. What does it mean to you to know that Christ shed His blood so that you could be dressed in His righteousness?

_____

_____

_____

_____

_____

_____

_____

Have you picked out a coming-home outfit or other special outfit for your little one yet? Tell him or her about it and why you picked it.

_____

_____

_____

_____

_____

_____

Hiccups

*I want you to know, brothers, that
what has happened to me has really
served to advance the gospel.*

PHILIPPIANS 1:12

*A*s I write this entry, there's a rhythmic thudding going on toward the very bottom of my belly: Baby's hiccups.

In our everyday slang we've borrowed the word *hiccup* from its medical usage to describe anything that comes along unexpectedly and disrupts the flow of things. We call it a hiccup when the computer suddenly stops working and then fixes itself, or when a flat tire deflates our plans for getting to the theater.

The apostle Paul had his fair share of life's hiccups. But when trumped-up charges landed him in prison, he didn't complain that he'd been thrown off course; he saw it as a way God was advancing His gospel. And indeed God used it to carry the gospel to the highest authorities, including Governor Felix, King Agrippa, and very likely Caesar himself, since it is clear that Paul appealed to Caesar and came to know Caesar's own household (Acts 9:15, 24:24, 25:12, 26:2, Philippians 4:22).

As we can see from Paul's life, nothing comes into our lives that surprises God. Nothing comes into our lives except by means of God allowing it. While God doesn't desire such things as sin, suffering, and disaster, He permits them (theologians call this His permissive will), and He works them together to bring about the good of His people and His kingdom. When we have confidence that God is at work in all things, it helps us relax and look expectantly for what He may be doing. So the next time your life seems to veer off course, just remember: in God's view, no hiccup is outside His plan.

Hiccups come in the form of minor inconveniences to major life-plan derailments. Are there any hiccups you've experienced lately? How may God actually be at work in them to advance His gospel or bring about a greater good?

_____

_____

_____

_____

_____

_____

Write a prayer for your little one to trust God during the minor and major disruptions of life and, moreover, to look expectantly for how God is at work in and through them.

_____

_____

_____

_____

_____

_____

Groaning for More

God heard their groaning and he
remembered his covenant with
Abraham, with Isaac and with Jacob.

EXODUS 2:24

Backaches, night wakings, discomfort, restlessness, fatigue—as pregnancy continues, discomfort has a way of making us ready for this stage of motherhood to be over. Any fears we may have about labor become displaced by a stronger desire to be done being pregnant. We groan for this phase to come to an end and for the next phase to begin.

The Israelites also experienced a deep yearning for their particular stage to be over. God told Abraham in Genesis, "Know for certain that your descendants will be strangers in a country not their own, and they will be enslaved and mistreated four hundred years" (15:13). Sure enough, the Israelites became slaves in Egypt, and as the harshness of their mistreatment increased, they groaned to be free. They groaned because they were meant for more. Likewise, as pregnant mothers we know that this stage is only temporary. We are meant for more: to love and cherish our babies in the flesh. All of this should remind us of an even deeper reality. If we feel discontent in this world, it is because we are pilgrims here. We are caught in time but destined for eternity. We were made for perfect relationship with God, but are currently rankled by our inconsistent fellowship with Him. We were made for a heavenly kingdom, not this temporary earthly one. Let your discontent lead you to groan for all God has made you to enjoy as you wait expectantly with thanksgiving. He is faithful.

What does it mean to live as strangers or pilgrims in this world? How should it motivate us to live godly lives?

_____

_____

_____

_____

_____

_____

_____

Are you ready to be done with pregnancy? What are you looking forward to most about the next stage?

_____

_____

_____

_____

_____

_____

_____

WEEK 37

The Wonder Within

*C*ongratulations! If your baby were born today, he or she would be considered full-term, and chances are good that your baby would not need any outside medical intervention. While babies will vary in size, by this week your little one weighs about 6.3 pounds and stretches between 18.9 and 20 inches long (about the length of a watermelon). So if your baby is full-term, what's he or she doing inside the womb? Your baby's continuing to practice those skills necessary for life outside your luxury, all-inclusive uterine hotel—things like sucking, swallowing, and sleeping. Something else to consider: you never know if your little one might need these extra few weeks to finish some vital lung development if by chance your due date is off.

How about you? How's Mama doing? Well, if you are like most pregnant women, by now you are quite miserable with the weight of the baby, the added aches and pains of the lower back and loose joints, and the insomnia that often strikes in the third trimester. Take some pressure off by getting in the tub or going for a swim. At the very least, rest and put your feet up (granted, it's hard with that nesting instinct in full gear). And while you've got your feet up, take some time to review the stages of labor and any notes you might have taken in your childbirth classes. Also take time to practice relaxing (something you'll need as contractions begin) and to pray over your upcoming labor.

POINTS FOR PRAYER AND PRAISE

Praise God that your baby has safely made it to full-term!

Pray for the final weeks (or perhaps days) of your baby's development. Pray that all systems will be mature and complete by the time your baby arrives. Pray also that one day, as your son or daughter grows, he or she will be brought to complete maturity in the faith.

Pray for yourself that labor will go smoothly and that you will be well rested and ready when it comes time.

MOMMY'S MEMORY VERSE

When [Jesus] saw the crowds, he had compassion on them, because they were harassed and helpless, like sheep without a shepherd.

MATTHEW 9:36

Date:

Birth Pains

*"Nation will rise against nation, and
kingdom against kingdom. There will be
famines and earthquakes in various places.
All these are the beginning of birth pains."*

MATTHEW 24:7–8

I went to bed last night with throbbing lower back pain and cramps that felt like bad menstrual cramps. This morning I woke up to the same, plus a lovely feeling of nausea. All day I wondered, *Is today the day?* With my first pregnancy, the back pain and cramps were the prelude to labor. But there's no way of knowing if this pregnancy will follow the same course or be entirely different. Either way, I'm confident that these pains signal progress is happening in my body toward the ultimate goal of delivering this baby and that the day will be here soon—whether that's *tonight* soon or four-weeks-from-now soon.

When Jesus addressed His disciples about the last days, He gave them some signs to watch for: wars, famines, earthquakes, persecution. He used the metaphor of birth pains to describe things that must happen before the end would come. And He encouraged His disciples not to be alarmed. Instead, He wanted them to be ready. And Jesus also wanted them to be encouraged that those days would not last forever (Matthew 24:22). God set limits to the duration of those events as they signal that the end—Christ's return—is at hand.

In this same passage Jesus told us that the gospel will be preached to the whole world and then the end will come (Matthew 24:14). Write a prayer for the advancement of the gospel to the ends of the earth, especially for those missionaries who are at work in the front lines of this advancement.

_____

_____

_____

_____

_____

_____

Even though Christ told us to expect extremely difficult times in the last days, He encouraged us that these days are numbered and that the glorious day of His coming will be soon. Likewise, as you experience early birth pains, say a prayer of thanks that Christ has set limits around the time they will last and that the glorious day of your baby's birth will be soon.

_____

_____

_____

_____

_____

_____

Received with Thanksgiving

Everything God created is good,
and nothing is to be rejected if it
is received with thanksgiving.

1 TIMOTHY 4:4

Nothing makes waiting seem less arduous than savoring the blessings of today!

As the days draw near for your little one's birth, savor the small things. This morning my husband got up early with our older son and I slept in until 9 a.m.! It felt amazing. Last night my mother-in-law babysat for us while we went on a date. And on Sunday I savored an entire worship service. These seem like small things, but I know that once the baby comes, it will be a while before I sleep through the night, go on a date with my husband, or enjoy a worship service without having to slip out to attend a fussy baby. My heart rejoices.

Yes, the discomforts grow as we reach the end of our pregnancy. Yes, my heart is bursting with excitement for the next stage. But today is a gift I don't want to miss. Now is a time to be lived for Christ. Today affords me the opportunity to make a difference, to make a memory, or to simply be still at the feet of Jesus and just enjoy Him. As you await the moment you will finally hold your little one, bless God for the gifts of this day. Lean into the present and ask Him how He wants to be glorified in you today.

What blessings do you have to be grateful for this day? List them and spend some time thanking God for His goodness.

_____

_____

_____

_____

_____

_____

_____

_____

What are a few things that you won't get to do for a while after the new baby arrives? Make plans to enjoy them now and make a point to rejoice in these days God has given you.

_____

_____

_____

_____

_____

_____

_____

_____

An Appointed Time

*"Is anything too hard for the LORD? I
will return to you at the appointed time
next year and Sarah will have a son."*

GENESIS 18:14

*A*s I write this, it's fewer than ten days until Christmas, and I'm thirty-seven weeks along. My midwife thinks this baby will come early as I'm already well dilated and effaced, and I've already been having lots of warm-up contractions. Everywhere I go people ask me when I want the baby to come: some suggest a Christmas baby, others say before the New Year for the tax break, and still others want me to hold out for the first baby of the New Year. Truth be told, I have no control over Baby's debut. As people ask, I tell them I want the baby to come in God's perfect timing, whatever day that may be.

In the midst of a season of waiting, it is comforting to know that God has an "appointed time" for your baby's arrival. Whether your water breaks in the middle of aisle seven at the local grocery or you have a date set for an induction, God appointed the time of this child's birth long before you even knew you were pregnant. He sees time at a glance; He sees all the birthdays your child will ever have; He sees all the contingencies of a lifetime and has chosen the perfect day, the appointed day, for the birth of your child. Rest in that.

Write a prayer asking God to help you wait patiently for the appointed day of your little one's arrival. Thank Him that He has carefully chosen that day and time.

_____

_____

_____

_____

_____

_____

_____

_____

Tell your baby a few details about your own birth day. What special birthdays in your growing-up years do you remember?

_____

_____

_____

_____

_____

_____

_____

_____

Spiritual Myopia

*When [Jesus] saw the crowds, he had
compassion on them, because they were harassed
and helpless, like sheep without a shepherd.*

MATTHEW 9:36

*P*regnancy—especially when we're this far along—has a way of making us incredibly self-focused. After all, there are the discomforts, the constant uncertainty as to when the baby will come, and the feeling that such a momentous time in one's life deserves to be the center of everyone's attention. In the midst of these kinds of feelings, we can easily overlook the needs of others.

We're given a different example, however, in the passion of our Lord Jesus Christ. In His hour of gravest need, at a time when no one would blame Him for being self-focused, He continued to minister to those around Him. Luke recorded a few details the other gospel writers didn't. In Luke 23:27–29 some women were following Jesus on His way to the cross, weeping and wailing for Him. He turned His compassion back on them, however. Luke alone recorded Jesus' famous words from the cross: "Father, forgive them, for they do not know what they are doing" (23:34). Luke also recorded the conversation between Jesus and the repentant thief on the cross next to Him. Jesus comforted him with the hope of paradise (23:43). Jesus saw others even in the midst of His pain. Ask God to give you spiritual eyes today like those of Jesus, eyes that look past your own situation to the needs of others.

In these incidents on Christ's way to Golgotha, and as He hung on the cross, we see how deep His compassion was for those whom He was sent to save. How can you focus your compassion on those around you even in the midst of your own difficult times?

_____

_____

_____

_____

_____

_____

_____

Write a prayer asking God to give your child a heart of compassion and to help make you a mother who continually models seeing and responding compassionately to those around her.

_____

_____

_____

_____

_____

_____

_____

WEEK 38

The Wonder Within

$\mathcal{Y}$our little wonder is approaching his or her full birth weight this week at around 6.8 pounds and stretching between 18.9 and 20 inches long (about the length of a watermelon). Inside the womb, the last-minute details of baby's growth continue, particularly in the brain. Here's an interesting fact for putting all this brain development into perspective: in the last eleven weeks in the womb, a baby typically doubles in weight, and in the last nine weeks in the womb, the brain also doubles in weight. This is mostly due to the protective covering called myelin. The outward folds and creases of this coating create the millions of neural pathways and connections needed for daily life and thought. And here's something else that's pretty fascinating: by the time your newborn arrives, his or her brain will be about a quarter of its ultimate size, but will already contain all the neurons it will ever have—close to 100 billion. Now that's one smart baby!

Speaking of intelligence, be wise about where you go in these last few weeks of pregnancy. Don't travel too far from where your hospital or birthing center is located. And if it's wintertime, make sure you've got a plan (and a snow shovel) for what to do if you go into labor during a big storm. If this is your first baby, it's likely that your labor won't be the fast and frantic kind you see portrayed in the movies; it more than likely will last about twelve to fifteen hours, giving you plenty of time and heads-up to get where you need to be. But of course you never know. Every labor is different and even some first-time labors can unfold rapidly, so be prepared!

POINTS FOR PRAYER AND PRAISE

- Praise God for good medical care and that you do not have to face labor and delivery alone.
- Pray for the connections being made in your baby's brain. Pray also for your son or daughter that, as he or she matures, connections will be made between the Bible and its applications to life.
- Pray that as you make plans for your birth experience, you will remember to submit them to the Lord and trust in His goodness even if things do not unfold as you have planned.

MOMMY'S MEMORY VERSE

Whatever happens, conduct yourselves in a manner worthy of the gospel of Christ.
PHILIPPIANS 1:27

Not According to Plan

Many are the plans in a man's heart, but
it is the LORD's purpose that prevails.

PROVERBS 19:21

*I*n a popular television comedy about a new mom, the series begins with the baby's birth. For the mom, who had carefully written and thought through her birth plan, absolutely nothing goes according to plan. As things go from bad to worse, the oft-repeated line in this episode is "This is *not* in the plan."

You've likely also given some thought to how you want the birth experience to unfold. Perhaps you've even drafted a birth plan—and if you haven't, it's a great idea to write one. But make sure that, as you draft your plans and prepare mentally for labor, you submit your plans to God.

Sometimes even our best, most well-intentioned plans are not God's. Perhaps you want a natural delivery, but will end up with a C-section because of circumstances out of your control. Perhaps you want an epidural, but end up laboring without one because labor happens so quickly or the anesthesiologist has trouble getting yours in.

We lay our plans, but God's purposes prevail. Sometimes His purposes involve thwarting evil that we cannot see. Sometimes He allows bad things to happen to us to further a good purpose that is beyond our vision. But whatever His purposes allow, you can trust that His plans are good and that He works *all* things together for good for those who believe in Him (Romans 8:28).

List some of the attributes of God that remind us that He is a God who is worthy of our surrender and trust.

_____

_____

_____

_____

_____

_____

_____

_____

What are some of your hopes and plans for the birth of your child? Why? As you write about them, surrender them to God in prayer. Trust His good heart toward you even if things do not go according to your plan.

_____

_____

_____

_____

_____

_____

_____

_____

Meditating on His Grace

I remember the days of long ago;
I meditate on all your works and
consider what your hands have done.

PSALM 143:5

*W*hat do you think of when you hear the word *meditation*? Perhaps it conjures up images of Eastern practices—cross-legged chanters trying to empty their minds. But while quite a few false religions and philosophies may have co-opted meditation, the practice is a thoroughly Christian tradition. Throughout the book of Psalms, David often mentions meditating on the laws of God (as in the verse above). Simply put, to meditate is to focus one's thoughts on something, to contemplate or reflect. And meditating on the Word of God is one of the best ways we can let His truths transform us.

In Psalm 143:5 David talked of meditating on the past deeds of God. As we contemplate the faithfulness of God in the past, we are naturally moved to trust more keenly in His future grace. After all, He is the same God yesterday, today, and tomorrow.

As the time of your due date draws near, take time to practice meditating on the Word of God. Meditating on His promises, His character, and His peace can help quiet your soul and ease your mind on your delivery day and on those disquieting days of pre-labor. Learning to focus your thoughts on God's Word is a discipline God will continue to use in your life to help you draw nearer to Him and become more like Him.

If meditating is new to you, an easy way to begin is to pick out a verse that brings you particular comfort and write it in the space below. Then tune out other distractions and read over the verse before you. Ask God to help you hear the things He is saying directly to you and to transform you through their meaning and power.

_____

_____

_____

_____

_____

_____

Isaiah 26:3 says, "You will keep in perfect peace him whose mind is steadfast, because he trusts in you." Meditate on this verse, especially in conjunction with any fears you may have about labor or life with a new baby. Write any insights God gives you during your time of meditation.

_____

_____

_____

_____

_____

_____

_____

Not Carte Blanche

Whatever happens, conduct yourselves in
a manner worthy of the gospel of Christ.

PHILIPPIANS 1:27

*W*hen it comes to Hollywood movie labor scenes, you can bet on a few common denominators: a woman who is a total basket case, a man who is a bumbling idiot, a labor that lasts no longer than the time it takes to change a flat tire, and a newborn who easily looks six months old. Movies are not the way to get educated on labor. They also reinforce the idea that pain gives women carte blanche to treat anyone around them with contempt.

While there's nothing like pain to bring out the worst in us, it's definitely not something to which we should aspire. In Eusebius's early church history, we see numerous accounts of the persecution inflicted upon early Christians: men and women who faced imprisonment, death before jeering crowds in the Colosseum, or being dragged naked through the streets. And yet those followers refused to renounce Christ.[10] Paul's words to the Philippians invoke pictures of persecution like the historian Eusebius described. Paul exhorted those believers to live worthy of the gospel.

Don't let the reference scare you: your labor will not be as painful as what those persecuted early Christians faced. But you can still pray for the grace to—despite pain and hardship—conduct yourself in a manner worthy of the gospel. May the words that come out of your mouth and your attitude toward your husband, nurses, and doctors all befit the name of Christ.

What biblical models do we have of men and women who conducted themselves with grace despite physical pain or psychological hardship?

_____

_____

_____

_____

_____

_____

_____

Write a prayer for your labor and delivery. Pray not only for a smooth delivery and healthy baby but also that whatever happens, you will conduct yourself in a manner worthy of the gospel.

_____

_____

_____

_____

_____

_____

_____

Desiring Closeness

The eternal God is your refuge, and
underneath are the everlasting arms.

DEUTERONOMY 33:27

*H*ave you thought about those precious first hours with your newborn? If possible, try to have as much skin-to-skin contact as possible. Studies show that babies with skin-to-skin contact after birth have a more stable temperature and heart rate, and a more successful latch if breast-feeding. One study found that a baby held skin-to-skin with a mother in the first ninety minutes of life was unlikely to cry, while a baby swaddled in a bassinet in those same first ninety minutes would cry about twenty to forty seconds of every five-minute interval. Your baby already knows the sound of your voice and the rhythm of your breathing, and craves closeness with you.

Like a newborn baby, we also crave closeness with God. When we are near Him, we not only feel safe, but we are safe. He is our refuge. He wraps us in His everlasting arms of love. He invites us to draw near to Him, and He promises that He in turn will draw near to us (James 4:8). He commands us to abide in Him (John 15:7, 9). And we see that He longs to gather us into His arms, both in how Jesus beckoned the little children to come (Mark 10:14–16) and in His words about His longing to gather Jerusalem under His wings (Matthew 23:37). Nuzzle into the arms of your Father today; you need that closeness as much as your newborn will need closeness with you.

The Bible frequently uses imagery of the arms of God and of His people hiding under the shelter of His wings. How do such images make you feel?

_____

_____

_____

_____

_____

_____

_____

Describe your hopes for the first few hours with your newborn. (Even most mandatory procedures—like vitamin K shots or eye drops—can be safely delayed for a bit while Mom and Baby have some bonding time.)

_____

_____

_____

_____

_____

_____

WEEK 39

The Wonder Within

By now your baby has reached his or her approximate birth weight, usually ranging somewhere between 6 and 9 pounds, and is 18.9 to 20 inches long (about the length of a watermelon—no wonder you feel so big!). Here's something interesting about your amazing soon-to-be newborn: many scientists now believe that the fetus initiates labor through the release of certain hormones that begin a kind of chain reaction. Of course God is the ultimate initiator, but isn't it amazing to think He may let your baby play some role in the complex choreography of your body bringing forth labor?

Speaking of when that baby of yours will come, here's something important to know: your due date is simply an educated guess based on a likely window of when you conceived. Less than 10 percent of babies are born on their due dates. One well-regarded study found that the average arrival of Baby came five days after the estimated due date for first-time moms and two days after the estimated due date for those who had given birth before. Suffice it to say, God holds the timing of all things under His perfect and wise control. And He knows exactly when your baby will come.

Points for Prayer and Praise

🔔 Praise God that His timing is perfect and that He has an appointed time for your baby's arrival.

🔔 Pray for your little one as he or she enters the world. Pray that God will keep your baby safe both in the first days of life and in all the days He has appointed for him or her.

🔔 Pray for yourself that you will lean on God and draw upon His strength and comfort during pre-labor, labor, and delivery.

Mommy's Memory Verse

Yes, Lord, walking in the way of your laws, we wait for you; your name and renown are the desire of our hearts.

Isaiah 26:8

Self-Doubt

*I pray also that the eyes of your heart may be
enlightened in order that you may know . . .
his incomparably great power for us who
believe. That power is like the working of
his mighty strength, which he exerted in
Christ when he raised him from the dead.*

EPHESIANS 1:18–20

As the day draws nearer for delivery, do you ever find yourself wondering, "Do I really have what it takes to be a mom?" Maybe this is not your first baby, but the idea of adding another child to the responsibilities you already have seems overwhelming. I find myself wrestling with this question often. Self-doubt rears its ugly head at the most inopportune times. It can paralyze us from walking out in faith into our calling.

When I look to the Scriptures for help on this question, God never points me back to my own strength. He always points me to the fact that Christ is alive in me. He points me to the fact that the strength that is available to me is the same mighty power that raised Christ from the dead. This is the power of Christ alive in me. When I look to my own strength, I get discouraged, but when I look to all that God has made available to me through Christ, how can I continue to doubt? To despair of my strength is fitting, but to despair of His strength is sin and folly.

In what aspects of motherhood do you find yourself most plagued with self-doubt? How can you find Christ to be your strength in those specific areas?

_____

_____

_____

_____

_____

_____

_____

_____

Which is more important: for your child to one day look back and think, "Man, my mom really had it together!" or to one day say, "My mom really showed me how to depend on Jesus!"? Why?

_____

_____

_____

_____

_____

_____

_____

_____

Worship in the Waiting

*Yes, Lord, walking in the way of your
laws, we wait for you; your name and
renown are the desire of our hearts.*

ISAIAH 26:8

As the due date draws nearer, somehow it seems the waiting gets harder. It's a Christmastime kind of excitement, knowing that in just a few short weeks (days? hours?) you will receive such a precious gift. But there's also anxiety in the interim as labor holds its own question marks. So how do you live well in the waiting?

One of my favorite verses on waiting is Isaiah 26:8. I particularly love this verse because it tells us what our posture should be as we wait. Even though waiting is a passive act, this is not a passive verse. As we wait, we are "walking in the way of [God's] laws." We are not idle. We are living the life He intended for us to live: loving others as ourselves, spreading His good news, honoring Him by living within the law's limits, using our gifts to bless others. Not only does this verse tell us how we should wait, but it also points to the end goal of why we wait on God: "your name and renown are the desire of our hearts." As you wait, meditate on this verse. Have you given your child to the Lord? Is your heartfelt desire for God's name and renown to be magnified through his or her life? Pray to this end.

How can you glorify God today as you wait for your child's entrance into the world? Do you need to turn your eyes away from yourself and to His kingdom purposes?

_____

_____

_____

_____

_____

_____

Write a prayer for your baby and the man or woman he or she will someday become. Ask that God's name and renown would be exalted in his or her life and that this will be the desire of your child's heart.

_____

_____

_____

_____

_____

_____

Love's Limits

"I made the sand a boundary for the sea,
an everlasting barrier it cannot cross. The
waves may roll, but they cannot prevail;
they may roar, but they cannot cross it."

JEREMIAH 5:22

For us, the sea is often an image of tranquility, rest, and relaxation. But in ancient Hebrew culture, the sea was at best a symbol of confusion and at worst a symbol of evil (Exodus 15:19, Isaiah 57:20, Luke 21:25, Jude v. 13). In the book of Jeremiah, we see something quite comforting: God has placed boundaries around how far the sea can go. The sand limits the sea. The waves roar and rush in, but they can only come so far. What a reassuring thought! While God may allow the repercussions of the fall, He puts limits on how far they can go.

When I think about the difficulty of labor, this verse comforts me. Because of the fall, pain is a part of childbirth (Genesis 3:16). But because of God's mercy, He puts limits on the amount of pain He will let us endure. There are lines the sea cannot cross. The waves may roar, but they will not prevail. And because we walk with Jesus, we will not face any trial without His protective presence. As the book of Isaiah tells us, "When you pass through the waters, I will be with you; and when you pass through the rivers, they will not sweep over you" (43:2). We are not to be afraid; God is with us (Isaiah 43:5).

We do not live in a world where evil, pain, and suffering have free reign. How does this thought comfort you?

_____

_____

_____

_____

_____

_____

_____

Which promises from Scripture will you set your mind on when the waves of labor seem unbearable?

_____

_____

_____

_____

_____

_____

_____

Rest

In vain you rise early and stay up
late, toiling for food to eat—for
he grants sleep to those he loves.

PSALM 127:2

*I*n the final weeks of pregnancy, sleep is elusive: night-wakings, pre-labor, and anxiety can keep you tossing and turning. And if the nesting instinct is in high gear, you may be scrubbing the floors and organizing the sock drawer at midnight. But as delivery day draws near, make getting rest a priority even if you don't feel like resting. You will need it for labor and the sleep-deprived days ahead.

I tend to burn the candle at both ends. I have a hard time turning in when something isn't finished. I have to remind myself often of the passage above. Part of the discipline of trusting the Lord is trusting that He has given us exactly the hours we need to do the tasks *He* wants us to do. When we go to bed at a reasonable time or even take a nap as the day of the birth draws near, we are resting in His grace instead of moving in our power. "Unless the LORD builds the house, its builders labor in vain" (Psalm 127:1). Even Jesus moved within the limits of a twenty-four-hour day. Certainly He could have worked later or gotten up earlier to heal one more or teach another parable, but He trusted in God who put limits on His physical body. How much more should we trust God with leaving things undone! He is in control. And rest is His gift to us.

Meditate for a few minutes on the limits of time that Jesus Himself lived and worked within when He lived on this earth. His formal ministry was limited to three short years. What insights do you glean from this? Can you trust God with your own time limitations?

_____

_____

_____

_____

_____

_____

_____

As women we often try to do it all. Sometimes it takes relinquishing our own desires for perfection, approval, or control to relax and rest. What is God asking you to relinquish in order for you to truly rest?

_____

_____

_____

_____

_____

_____

_____

WEEK 40

The Wonder Within

*H*ooray! The finish line is well within sight. Congratulations on making it this far in your expectant journey. Soon you should be holding that precious little one in your arms. You can expect him or her to weigh about 7 to 9 pounds and stretch between 18 and 21 inches long (about the size of . . . a newborn baby, of course!). And when your long-awaited one arrives, he or she will already have quite a few skills—grasping, sucking, and startling reflexes that he or she perfected in the womb.

And how's Mom doing this week? Likely, by now you are having some pre-labor symptoms. Take heart. Many of these pains are helping your body get ready for delivery. Your cervix is likely softening, and many moms will be dilated a few centimeters before labor even begins. If the baby's head is down, the pressure of his head on your cervix will also help to move this process along. Pay attention for signs of labor. Obviously, if your water breaks or contractions begin fast and furiously, call your practitioner. But also be prepared for more subtle symptoms that often are a tip-off that labor is a few days or hours away—things like losing your mucous plug, lower back pain, or even a sudden burst of energy. Do your body a favor and, as you wait, make sure to rest up. You never know what time of day (or night!) labor may begin.

Points for Prayer and Praise

- Praise God for bringing you and Baby safely to the end of your pregnancy!

- Pray for your little one as he or she arrives that all vital signs will be strong. And pray for his or her spiritual vitality in the years to come.

- Pray for yourself that God will give you peace, patience, and joy as you face the final countdown to Baby and that you will also walk in His strength in the exhausting and wonderful days of life with a newborn.

Mommy's Memory Verse

How can we thank God enough for you in return for all the joy we have in the presence of our God because of you?

1 THESSALONIANS 3:9

Forgoing Fear

*Cast all your anxiety on him
because he cares for you.*

1 PETER 5:7

*A*s D-Day approaches, it's only natural to find your thoughts often turning anxiously to what labor will be like. But the Bible commands us repeatedly not to be anxious or afraid (Matthew 6:25, John 14:27, Philippians 4:6). Why? We have a good God who is utterly trustworthy, cares for us, and promises to work all things together for the good of those who love Him and are called according to His purposes (Romans 8:28). When we dwell on our anxious thoughts, our hearts are not reflecting the truth of who He is. While inevitably there will be real and often overwhelming challenges in our lives, God doesn't want us to wallow in our worry, but instead bring those cares to Him in prayer.

Interestingly enough, in labor, fear is not only unhelpful but also counterproductive. When we are anxious, our muscles tighten, our breathing becomes shallow, and our heart rate accelerates. In labor, the uterus has a harder time doing what it is meant to do when anxiety tightens other muscles and diverts oxygen and blood flow elsewhere. In fact, anxiety can sometimes stall labor altogether. So as you prepare for labor, cast all your anxieties upon the Lord: He cares for you, and He *will* care for your every need as this little life comes into the world.

Do you have a hard time applying the Bible's commands on worry and anxiety? How do you think you can make prayer a more reflexive response to your anxious thoughts?

_____

_____

_____

_____

_____

_____

Take some time to pray through any anxieties you have about labor. Write down any ways that God encourages your heart or your mind as a result.

_____

_____

_____

_____

_____

_____

Framed in His Goodness

The people grew impatient on the way;
they spoke against God and against
Moses, and said, "Why have you brought
us up out of Egypt to die in the desert?
There is no bread! There is no water!
And we detest this miserable food!"

NUMBERS 21:4–5

*H*ave you had that baby yet?" What more ridiculous question could people ask you? Obviously not! Between the baby's head pushing down into your pelvis, the sharp pains that take your breath away, and your constant need to run to the bathroom, it's no wonder you are impatient for Baby's arrival. But while it's easy to complain, we must remember that behind us and before us is the grace of God.

The Israelites often had complaining hearts. In this passage in Numbers, God had given them victory over a group of Canaanites, had provided food and water for them in the wilderness, and had promised to give them ultimate victory over their enemies as well as a land flowing with milk and honey. And yet they complained. Not only did they complain, they questioned God's character. Had He not shown Himself to be all-gracious and all-powerful? Their lives were framed in His goodness—goodness behind them, goodness before them—but they didn't trust God in the moment. Remember, God has framed your days with His goodness. He has given you the gift of this pregnancy. His grace goes before you. Trust in His timing. Give Him the gift of a grateful and patient heart.

What promises do we have from God that He will be with us in the days to come and give us all that we need?

_____

_____

_____

_____

_____

_____

_____

_____

Write a prayer for a smooth and healthy delivery of your little one. Pray also for the grace to live in the present with a grateful and patient heart.

_____

_____

_____

_____

_____

_____

_____

_____

Words Fail

*How can we thank God enough for you
in return for all the joy we have in the
presence of our God because of you?*

1 Thessalonians 3:9

The day is drawing near. You'll nuzzle that soft little head underneath your chin, kiss those sweet cheeks, and feel those tiny little fingers curling around your own. Stroking baby feet, smelling baby skin, watching those little sleep-smiles flicker across the face of your little one mid-dream—there are few greater joys than those of a new baby. Your heart will swell in gratitude and you'll say with the apostle Paul, "How can we thank God enough for you in return for all the joy we have in the presence of our God because of you?"

But while that joy runs deep, keep fixed in mind an even greater joy, one that will not be immediate but will be eternal. When Paul wondered how he could thank God enough for the joy he had in his heart, it was because of seeing the Thessalonians, his spiritual children, mature in their faith. He wrote, "Now we really live, since you are standing firm in the Lord" (1 Thessalonians 3:8). While you can't change your children's hearts, you can pray and work and sacrifice with this hope in mind: that one day your children will stand firm in Christ while bearing fruit and bringing Him glory. What joy you will have in the presence of God then! How sweet it is to sacrifice for such a beautiful sight!

Imagine what it will be like to one day stand in heaven side by side with all the children for whom you have prayed and sacrificed, loved and taught. While only God can change hearts, He certainly uses parents as a primary means of bringing the gospel and sanctification to His little ones. Write a prayer that God may use you in this glorious task of bringing your children to know Him.

_____

_____

_____

_____

_____

_____

Take time to thank God for the joy you have in His presence because of this child you are carrying. Record now what you are feeling as you think of the prospect of finally meeting your precious one.

_____

_____

_____

_____

_____

_____

_____

Lips to Praise

I will extol the LORD at all times; his
praise will always be on my lips.

PSALM 34:1

$\mathcal{W}$hat is on your lips today? Is it praise?

Chances are, if you are still reading along in this devotional, you haven't yet had your baby. (That's perfectly normal by the way!) Amidst the irritating comments like "You look as big as a house!" and the generally lousy way you are feeling right now, there's a pretty good chance that praise isn't the first thing on your lips. But let David's words challenge you: "I will extol the LORD at *all* times; his praise will *always* be on my lips" (Psalm 34:1, italics mine).

So what will it look like today and in the weeks ahead to have His praise continually on your lips? Here's a glimpse:

> I will extol the Lord while waiting for this baby to come, while in the throes of labor, and when finally holding this gift in my arms. I will extol the Lord amidst sleep deprivation, diaper blowouts, spit-up, hormone changes, and 2 a.m. feedings. I will extol the Lord for newborn nuzzles, first coos, and sweet smiles. I will extol the Lord when none of my clothes fit and I'm desperate for a night out. In the days of tiny fingers curling around my own and a downy head tucked beneath my chin and in the days of desperately needing coffee, my lips will continually sing His praise.

How can you remind yourself to have God's praise continually on your lips today and in the days ahead? Could you put a sticky note on the mirror, tie a ribbon around your wrist, or even write out a copy of this verse and tuck it in your hospital bag? Brainstorm some ways to put the words of the psalmist into action and write your plan here.

_____

_____

_____

_____

_____

_____

Dear Little One,

As I wait to finally meet you, I want you to know . . .

_____

_____

_____

_____

_____

_____

Epilogue

The warm water of the tub helped me relax through the rhythmic tightening of contractions. I closed my eyes and tried to release the tension in my shoulders. I'd asked my husband to turn out the harsh fluorescent lights of the hospital bathroom and just keep the door open to the labor room. So while the room itself was dark, each time I opened my eyes I'd see the light of that wintry morning streaming through the window just outside my door.

As I concentrated on the morning light, three words kept running through my head. As the pain came and went, first with long intervals and then with hardly a moment for me to recoup, I kept silently repeating the words *dar a luz*. This Spanish phrase for giving birth literally means "to bring or to give to the light." I silently prayed for God's strength and help as I told Him I was ready to bring this child to the light.

I'm still not sure why that phrase was on my laboring lips (seven years of Spanish classes don't exactly a native speaker make). But as I mull over it today, slouched down in my glider rocker, laptop open, week-and-a-half-old Isaiah Andrew Larson happily asleep on my chest, I can't help but think about that phrase from a spiritual point of view.

The world that our little ones enter into is a world not of light but of great darkness. It breaks the heart of every mother to think of the pain, frustration, injustice, sickness, and evil that our children will one day encounter. We would do anything to spare them such heartache. But while we can't spare them the darkness, we can partner with the Holy Spirit as we seek to bring them into God's light.

The day-to-day life of a mother often involves a series of menial and mundane tasks. But in the midst of those ordinary moments—bending our bodies to pull clothes off a toddler in full-throttle tantrum minutes before bath time, kneeling to kiss a skinned knee, or lifting a wiggling child to pretend plane through the air for just one more giggle—we labor in the spiritual realm to bring our children to the light. We discipline; we love; we laugh; but we are always teaching them about the Lord—His righteous standards, His never-ending love, His joy in His creation. And it is here, in the midst of this labor, that we worship God with our lives. Bending, kneeling, and lift arms in holy worship, not in cathedrals or simply on Sunday mornings, but in the ordinary messiness and exuberance of daily life. In the midst of both the pain and the exaltation of our labor as mothers, we worship. We cooperate with the Holy Spirit in hope and in faith that we might bring our children out of darkness and into His glorious light.

Record your birth story here. How was God's faithfulness evident?

_____

_____

_____

_____

_____

_____

_____

_____

What name did you decide on for your little one? Is there any special significance?

Write a prayer for yourself and your little one that as he or she grows, you will continue to co-labor with God to bring your child into His glorious light.

_____

_____

_____

_____

_____

_____

_____

_____

_____

_____

_____

_____

_____

_____

_____

_____

How have you grown in your understanding of God and motherhood in these past nine months? What insights or experiences are you grateful to have had?

_____

_____

_____

_____

_____

_____

_____

_____

_____

_____

_____

_____

_____

_____

_____

_____

_____

Your Baby: A Week-by-Week Stroll Up the Produce Aisle

Week 5 Pomegranate Seed 0.13 inches

Week 6 Sweet Pea 0.25 inches

Week 7 Blueberry 0.51 inches

Week 8 Raspberry 0.63 inches and 0.04 ounces

Week 9 Cherry 0.9 inches and 0.07 ounces

Week 10 Grape 1.2 inches and 0.14 ounces

Week 11 Lime 1.6 inches and 0.25 ounces

Week 12 Clementine 2.1 inches and 0.49 ounces

Week 13 Peach 2.9 inches and 0.81 ounces

Week 14 Apple 3.5 inches and 1.5 ounces

Week 15 Navel Orange 4 inches and 2.5 ounces

Week 16 Avocado 4.6 inches and 3.5 ounces

Week 17 Sweet Onion 5.1 inches and 5.9 ounces

Week 18 Sweet Potato 5.6 inches and 6.7 ounces

Week 19 Mango 6 inches and 8.5 ounces

Week 20 Banana 10 inches (crown to heel*) and 10.6 ounces

Week 21 Carrot 10.5 inches and 12.7 ounces

Week 22 Cucumber 10.9 inches and 15.17 ounces

Week 23 Eggplant 11.38 inches and 1.10 pounds

Week 24 Corn 11.81 inches and 1.32 pounds

Weeks 25–28 Romaine Lettuce 13.6 to 14.8 inches and
    1.46 to 2.22 pounds

Weeks 29–32 Pineapple 15.2 to 16.7 inches and 2.5 to 3.75 pounds

Weeks 33–36 Leeks 17.2 to 18.7 inches and 4.2 to 5.7 pounds

Weeks 37–39 Watermelon 18.9 to 20 inches and 6.3 to 7.25 pounds

Week 40 A NEWBORN BABY! 18 to 21 inches and 7 to 9 pounds

*For weeks 5 through 19, length measurements are from crown to rump. For weeks 20 through 40, length measurements are from crown to heel. All measurements are averages and your little one's true measurements may vary.

Acknowledgments

A few days ago it dawned on me that writing this book, like the expectant journey it details, has taken me exactly nine months (from October 1, 2011 to July 1, 2012). Through the seasons of writing—from being great with my second child, to cuddling a newborn, to watching first smiles and rolls—this book has come to life. And with so much change happening in my own life, this book wouldn't have been possible without the love and support of so many family, friends, and colleagues.

I'm grateful to my husband, Mark, who encouraged the idea of this book from its conception and did not let the fact that we'd soon be adding to our own family daunt him or keep me from what God was calling me to write. My first expectant journey with my son, Luke, was, of course, much of the inspiration behind this book. Those days of wonder, joy, and hope made this book a twinkle in my eye. My newest addition, Isaiah, gave his mama the kick (from utero) that she needed to get this book started, and continued to open her eyes to the wonders of new life.

The prayers of my church, Potomac Hills Presbyterian, and more specifically the elders, my women's small group, and my husband's accountability group, undergirded my daily writing.

In the final push to completion, many cheered me as I labored. I'm grateful for Lori Smith, always an enthusiastic coach and friend who stood by my side, especially on the hard days. Babysitting help from my mother-in-law, Diane Winter, as well as Andi Lawson, Rachel

Luckenbaugh, and Emma and Sophia Cliffton who helped free me up in the final countdown to completion.

My mother, Sally Claire, was the first to read this book and, like any good doting (and generous) grandparent, told me there was not one flaw in it. (Thankfully, more objective voices would follow.) The enthusiasm of my father, Earl Claire, brothers, Dan and David Claire, and their wives, Elise and Amy Claire, also helped welcome this book into the world.

The able hands of the ever-approachable Lisa Stilwell, my editor at Thomas Nelson, helped to deliver this book to the public in tip-top shape. My midwife and friend, Courtney Hasseman, CNM, also checked this book, especially the developmental pages, for accuracy. And my agent, Andrea Heinecke of Alive Communications, was my advocate and adviser throughout.

It's with an eager heart that I now look forward in gratitude to those who will help this book's influence grow.

Finally, this book would not exist at all if it weren't for the daily inspiration and empowerment of my Lord and Savior Jesus Christ, who honors me with the privilege of ascribing Him glory by being a scribe for Him.

A Challenge and an Invitation

If you've read this book and it has blessed you, consider blessing another expectant mother by giving her a copy or recommending it early in her journey. And for more of my writing or to find other like-minded moms to walk the journey of faith alongside, sign up for my mailing list and join the conversation at my website www.CatherineClaireLarson.com, friend my Facebook page Catherine Claire Larson, or follow me on Twitter @CatherineLarson. Thanks for reading, and my prayers go with you that this book would deeply impact not only your life for Christ but also the life of your child to the glory and praise of God.

Endnotes

1. *The Book of Common Prayer* (New York: Oxford University Press, 2005), 361.
2. Saint Augustine, *The Confessions* (New York: Oxford University Press, 2009), 3.
3. Quoted in William D. Pederson, *Presidential Profiles: The FDR Years* (New York: Infobase Publishing, 2006), 334.
4. Quoted in Herb Galewitz, ed., *Mother: A Book of Quotations* (Mineola, NY: Dover Publications, 2002), 24.
5. William Ross Wallace, "The Hand That Rocks the Cradle Is the Hand That Rules the World," http://www.theotherpages.org/poems/wallace1.html.
6. Elisabeth Elliot, *A Chance to Die: The Life and Legacy of Amy Carmichael* (Grand Rapids, MI: Revell Books, 2005).
7. Bridget Coila, "Memory Development in Babies," *Livestrong.com*, May 3, 2011, http://www.livestrong.com/article/95646-memory-development-babies/.
8. See Phillips Russell, *Benjamin Franklin: The First Civilized American* (New York: Cosimo, 2005), 138.
9. Jennifer Daniels, "Tattoo," *Summer Filled Sky*, TNtrees Music, June 25, 2004, compact disc.
10. *Eusebius: The Church History*, trans. Paul L. Maier (Grand Rapids, MI: Kregel Publications, 2007).

Notes